MW00944345

The Score's Wrong

The Lunatic Rantings of
a Volleyball Dad

by
Thomas J. Wurtz

authorHOUSE®

AuthorHouse™
1663 Liberty Drive, Suite 200
Bloomington, IN 47403
www.authorhouse.com
Phone: 1-800-839-8640

First published by AuthorHouse 11/5/2007

ISBN: 978-1-4343-4757-2 (sc)

Library of Congress Control Number: 2007908323

Printed in the United States of America
Bloomington, Indiana

This book is printed on acid-free paper.

Dedication

This book is dedicated to my wife, Barb,
my three daughters, Sara, Rachel and Danielle.
Please forgive me for writing this book,
for I know not what I am doing.

Contents

Dramatic Introduction

It is July 5th. I am sitting on a Delta jet waiting to fly from Salt Lake City to the Northern Kentucky/Greater Cincinnati International Airport. My blood pressure has dropped to 225 over 180 and my pulse rate has plummeted to just over 100. I start to realize that I will be okay. I made it. I was one of the lucky ones. There are many people who have experienced this tragic lifestyle and are now residing in an insane asylum. I take a deep breath and I rest my head on the comfortable coach seat. I thank God for my good fortune. I begin to smile and look forward to getting my life back to normal.

Wow! What a dramatic opening for a stupid book about the stupid sport of volleyball. Allow me to bring you up to date. For the past four days my sixteen-year-old daughter, Danielle, has participated in the National Junior Olympic Volleyball Tournament in Salt Lake City. We are preparing to journey home as the tournament and volleyball season is finally over. Overall, the national tournament was a huge success. Success in the world of club volleyball simply means that not a single parent went "postal," and no one ended up in jail. We did experience the normal events usually found at a volleyball tournament – plumbing explosions, food poisoning, hair dryers catching on fire, players crying and parents wanting to cry. If you have never been to a national volleyball tournament, it closely resembles an adult prison environment. The coach decides when you are to leave the hotel, when you are to eat, where you will eat and what time you will go to bed. On this glorious day, I felt the sweet taste of freedom as the volleyball warden will no longer control my every move.

This year's trip to the national tournament started out very bizarre. When my wife, daughter and I arrived at the airport, there was a problem with my airline ticket. Since I used a previous airline credit to purchase my ticket, the simple process of checking-in was now very complicated. The skycap was having a difficult time locating my ticket in the computer system. In the spirit of assisting the skycap, my wife pulled out her documentation and produced my ticket number and stated to the skycap, "I don't know how your system works, but I have the ticket number for my husband." The skycap shot back, "Ma'am, I know how our system works, will you please just shut up?" My wife and I were stunned that he told her to "shut up." Being a good husband, I quickly fantasized as to how good that must have felt for the skycap. Every husband who witnessed this scene was busy giving high fives to each other. As we walked away after the matter was finally resolved, I high fived the skycap (behind my wife's back) and slipped him a $50 dollar tip for allowing me to experience one of my life's fantasies. I know I should have defended my wife's honor and confronted the skycap by shouting, "Hey, don't you talk to my wife the way she talks to me!" However, I stood there in a state of shock and said nothing. How could something so wrong feel so good?

We landed in Salt Lake City about three hours later. It was a beautiful day and the temperature was around 125 degrees. It was hot. As Rodney Dangerfield would say, "It was so hot I actually saw three improperly hydrated young girls burst into flames." It was a great beginning to our trip, but I knew the best was yet to come. Barb and I mentally prepared ourselves for four days of volleyball excitement and drama. After watching countless volleyball matches over the four days, I concluded that this year's tournament featured many of the Incredible Hulk's children. I saw sixteen-year-old girls that were six-feet-five and a few, I swear, shaving between matches. I don't know if young girls take steroids, but I did encourage the officials to test many of the players. Several of the girls' voices were deeper than my voice and that scared the hell out of me.

Let me properly introduce myself. My name is Tom Wurtz and I am a recovering volleyball parent. For the past ten years, my daughters have participated in the world of "club volleyball." Club volleyball is a team of girls from many different schools who are selected to compete at a national level. Usually, only the best of the best compete at this level unless politics, weaseling and conniving parents and coaches are involved. I know many of you are dealing with similar diseases from other select sports such as baseball, basketball, hockey, soccer, swimming or dance. If your child is caught up in the world of "club whatever," you will be able to relate to my disease and my story. My story is not pretty. If you suffer from a weak stomach or have a tendency to become offended easily, this book is not for you. May I suggest you read something that is a lot less vulgar and disgusting, such as *The Exorcist*. You have been warned.

For the past ten years, I have allowed myself to be infected with V.D. (volleyball disease). This mentally destructive disease can, and will, cause anxiety, stress, explosive outbursts and extreme depression. Some volleyball parents may even experience bi-polar symptoms. (I never understood what bi-sexual polar bears had to do with their condition.) Anyway, all of these emotional conditions will occur in the first week of a typical volleyball season. One of the symptoms will cause everyone it touches to speak in a low-voice to another volleyball parent so the volleyball gods will not hear their heresy. Whenever you walk by two volleyball parents engaged in a low-voice conversation, and they immediately stop talking when you approach, I can assure you that the topic being discussed is club volleyball. I have attempted self-treatment for many years; however, the disease has refused to go into remission. I have tried volleyball shock therapy and medication, but it seems nothing will cure this nasty disease. On several occasions, I have come very close to checking myself into a V.A. (Volleyball Anonymous) treatment center. However, I know I can beat this disease in the long run. I know I must not give up and I must continue to fight for my mental survival.

I decided as part of my self-therapy treatment, I would write this book in an attempt to help other volleyball parents deal with this repulsive disease. I am not a professional writer, and my only goal is to share my deep-buried inner feelings about this disorder, so hopefully this emotional release will set us all free. I just realized that I'm starting to sound like Dr. Phil's love child. I probably should shut up, get off this couch, and get on with the book.

I hope you will enjoy this book, and I pray it brings you a short diversion from the world of club volleyball or a short diversion from life's challenges. Before we get started, let me share with you one of my favorite volleyball cheers. For some reason, the acts of cheerleading and volleyball are very closely related. I have attended many volleyball tournaments and thought a cheerleading convention had broken out. I guess girls just like to cheer. I have never attended a boy's basketball game where the players call time out and begin to recite an organized cheer. I guess boys and girls are different after all. Anyway, one of my daughter's favorite volleyball cheers goes like this, "Mirror, mirror on the wall, pretty girls don't play volleyball so let's get ugly!" I agree. It's time to get *real* ugly.

The Score's Wrong

If there is one thing that is consistent in the world of club volleyball it is clearly that the score, at some point in the match, will be wrong. This may sound strange if you have never experienced the world of club volleyball. Since I am one of those "passionate dads," my number one job at all tournaments was to follow the score on a point-by-point basis to make sure that we properly received all of our correct points. It was my job to yell out, "The score is wrong! The score is wrong!" I know I sounded a little like Paul Revere when he said, "The British are coming! The British are coming!" I have found that you must yell at *least* twice if you hope to get the referee's attention. My goal was to yell loud enough to wake-up the referee from their nap, therefore, you can't be timid when you yell, "The score is wrong!" You must act like you are being tortured, which most of the time I really wasn't acting.

If you are not familiar with the scorekeeping process in volleyball, let me fill you in. The scorekeeping in the world of club volleyball is managed by preteen and teenage players who are in-between their matches. Most of the tournaments use a format of "play, sit, play, scream, play, sit and cry." I think I have it correctly. Most of the refereeing is done by the volleyball players from other teams waiting to play their next match. The only adult involved in the refereeing process is called the "up-ref", or as I call them the "High Priest." The High Priest stands on a platform hovering on one side of the net. The High Priest signals the start of each point and calls many of the violations on the players. The High Priest does not keep score. I guess keeping score is beneath the almighty High Priest. The important responsibility of scorekeeping is done by "Ritalin-deprived volleyball kids." I have considered opening a Ritalin stand at each tournament, and I probably would become a millionaire. The score is usually wrong at least once in every match. How many sporting events do you go to where the score is constantly wrong? If you want the score to be correct, you need a parent to assume the roll of "screamer." This was the role that I played. It is not pretty, but someone must act like an idiot. I normally was the most qualified idiot among our parents.

It is so frustrating because many of these kids simply refuse to pay attention during the matches and continually miss points or give points to the wrong team. The parents are usually the first to notice the score is wrong and begin yelling, "the score is wrong" to the High Priest. The majority of the time the High Priest simply ignores the parents until we become out of control. If you are not insane when you arrive at a volleyball tournament, I will assure you that you will be when you arrive back on Planet Earth.

After several minutes of yelling, the High Priest will ask the Ritalin-deprived scorekeepers if the score is correct. Like clockwork they answer, "yes." The parents now consider storming the floor, and if we can make the High Priest uncomfortable enough, he/she will eventually descend from their throne and make their pilgrimage to the scorer's table. Once the High Priest comes down from the throne, we know we are in for a long delay. After several minutes, that seems like several hours, the High Priest concludes that the score is correct. The parents are now so upset that many will call Dr. Phil and attempt to be scheduled for therapy. I have never experienced a sport where the score is *constantly* in question. When did counting become so challenging for preteen and teenage kids?

Volleyball Dad Lesson #1
Live in the Now

What a great lesson for adults and kids! I have survived two massive heart attacks and I truly appreciate the concept of living in the "now." We live in such a fast-paced society that we are always worried about what we're going to do for entertainment next. Our minds are always taking us someplace else when we really just need to enjoy the "now." Our daughters worry about where they are going after the tournament, where we will be eating later and what activities we have planned for the evening. We are so concerned about the future that we waste our "now."

I really try to focus on enjoying the "now" time. When my daughters are playing volleyball, I focus 100% of my attention on the game. No cell phones and no distractions. I really enjoy the moment. I love watching my daughters compete and put forth their maximum effort. I realize the actual volleyball experience is not important, however, my girls did learn a very valuable lesson about life. If you want to even have a chance in life, you must commit to maximum effort. We cannot give half an effort and hope to succeed. I insist that my girls give maximum effort on the court, or I make it clear I am not a happy volleyball camper.

One of my daughters was playing in a match where our team was clearly the superior team. Everyone knew the match was a mismatch. Unfortunately, the girls quickly realized the match was going to be easy. My daughter got caught up in the relaxed atmosphere; she was laughing on the court and did not play to her full potential. After the easy win, I called my daughter aside and had a good old fashioned father-daughter talk. The kind of talk that is always difficult, but always necessary. I sternly scolded her for her lack of intensity and passion throughout the match. I stated that I had no intention of leaving work to watch her matches if that was going to be the amount of effort she was going to put forth. I then left and let my daughter come home with my wife.

My wife later told me that my daughter cried on and off for about two hours. She kept asking my wife, "Why is Dad so upset with me?" My wife repeated the same reasons I gave earlier. Since that conversation, I have never seen my daughter give less than 100% on the court. We all need to be reminded and held accountable for our actions. It is my responsibility to make sure my daughters reach their full potential. This is a responsibility I take very seriously. I want my daughters to understand that *winning isn't everything, but the effort to win is*. This philosophy is very important if we have any desire to accomplish anything in life. The quality of our daughters' lives will depend on the quality of their life's habits. I know all Volleyball Dads believe that bad habits will equal a bad life. It's best to break these habits when we're young, because the older we get, the more stubborn we become. I have been battling my bad habits and the consequences of those bad habits for 50 years. I know first-hand how hard it is to make a lifestyle change. I guess that is why I am so concerned when I notice bad habits entering my daughters' lives.

Volleyball Dad Lesson #2
Eliminate the Activity-High Syndrome

I believe our society has been conditioned to constantly focus on what we are going to do next. I am sure the kids refereeing the volleyball matches don't need Ritalin; they are simply conditioned to worry about what they are going to do tonight, tomorrow or this weekend. I wish I had a nickel for every time one of my daughters stated they were bored. We have more activities and distractions now than anytime in human history. How can we be bored? When I was young, we had three television stations and a few radio stations. Yes, I know I sound old by making these comments. Our children have four hundred television stations, numerous radio stations, computers, and a thousand other gadgets and yet they complain about being bored. Why? Because they are not bored, they are addicted to the next "activity high." Whatever they are doing now is considered boring and they believe the next activity will generate the desired high. I believe our children are addicted to mass activity. The more activities they participate in, the more activities they need to achieve their next highs.

Let's face it, we, as parents cause the majority of these problems. We encourage our kids to participate in every activity we know of. Many children play basketball, soccer, swimming, dance, music and hundreds of additional activities. We condition our children to constantly search for the next activity high. I have seen kids quit playing volleyball at age fifteen because they are burned out. It seems crazy to push kids so hard that they cry "uncle" so early in life. I believe as parents we need to look at what we are doing to our daughters. It's hard to justify our daughters having a nervous breakdown at age fifteen. Maybe we need to lighten up a little and enjoy our daughters while we can. Life happens so fast, I often wish my daughters would slow down and enjoy being young girls for awhile. As we know, being an adult sure can bring on a few challenges. We probably should let our children be children.

Caravanning Or "Idiots on Parade"

For the past thirty years, I have traveled throughout the country attending business meetings or vacationing. On many of these trips, I am required to fly on a plane <u>and</u> rent a car. I'm telling you the truth (I am not making this up.) I have always felt very confident that I would be able to locate and arrive at my destination on time. However, the volleyball gods do not believe in my ability to accomplish such a challenging task. Caravans, or "Idiots on Parade," as I called the tradition, are mandatory for all volleyball tournaments. This event is probably very similar to participating in the *Amazing Race* television show. On the show, participants show up at a common starting point and they must find their way to a distant location. They are given very little information and the confusion makes for a great television show. Volleyball caravans are much the same. The parents meet in a common location, and usually only one or two parents have the directions to the tournament. A few parents may know the name of the actual destination city. The rest of the parents must *lock-on* to the car ahead of them and hope they do not become separated from the lead idiot, as this is the car that leads the parade to our destination. Many parents believe they are the wingman from the movie *Top Gun,* and they refuse to be separated from the lead idiot. I have seen parents run red lights and even reach speeds in excess of eighty miles per hour in order to remain in the parade. After participating in this parade for many years, I honestly believe that if the lead car drove off the road into a ravine, all the remaining cars would follow.

I recently heard this story that illustrates the fun associated with the "Idiots on Parade" strategy. This parent was participating in the first tournament of the year for her daughter's club volleyball team. It is not unusual for a team to meet at a local mall or some other gathering spot at 5:30 a.m. Since the tournaments in club volleyball begin in January, it is very dark at 5:30 a.m. I was not aware that 5:30 a.m. even existed. I heard about 5:30 a.m. but I never experienced it first-hand. When this family arrived at the volleyball gathering ground, the mom asked her daughter if she recognized any of the players on her team. The daughter pointed to one player she thought was on her team, so the mom jockeyed for a position behind that player's car. The "Idiots on Parade" finally received clearance for take-off from the volleyball air-traffic controller, and the pilgrimage to their first tournament began. Approximately nine cars attempted to follow each other for the next sixty miles. That's not as easy as it sounds.

The dedicated mom diligently followed the car ahead of her as if her life depended on it. After a short time, the mom started to experience that "uh-oh" feeling. From the little information she received about the tournament, she thought they would be traveling to Oxford, Ohio. She quickly realized that her current path would not lead her there. The mom started a process called "thinking." This process is usually prohibited when you are participating in an officially sanctioned "Idiots on Parade" event, but she felt compelled to violate this critical rule. She concluded that they had mistakenly gotten in the wrong parade. She now realized that several volleyball teams had gathered at the same place. This was not the parade for her daughter's team. This team appears to be going to a tournament in Dayton, Ohio.

The mom now had a real problem. She not only realized that she was in the wrong parade, she was also stuck in the *middle* of the wrong parade. If she decided to exit the parade, the cars following her would now follow her and the rest of that team would end up in Oxford, not Dayton, Ohio. Being a true volleyball patriot, the mom stayed in the parade in order to make sure her followers ended up at the right tournament. Once she arrived in Dayton and was released from her parade duties, she quickly took off for Oxford. How she made it to Oxford is still a mystery, as no one has ever found a volleyball site on their own. The good news is that she did arrive at an acceptable time and her daughter was able to stop crying by noon and partake in the volleyball fun. The punishment for arriving late at a volleyball tournament is quite severe. When I was in shock-therapy, I heard about one volleyball player who arrived late for a tournament and was refrained from carrying her cell phone *during* a match. The ACLU had to step in and reinstate the player's constitutional right to the pursuit of cell phone happiness. As I told you earlier, this stuff can get very ugly.

At one of our very first volleyball tournaments, we lined up for our parade as instructed. We left Northern Kentucky and started to head north on I-75. So far, all is fine. Shortly thereafter, I notice something was wrong as we did not exit I-75 to get on I-74. Our stated path was to lead us to west I-74. This seemed odd, but we were engaged in an official "Idiots on Parade" ritual, so no one broke out of the formation. We then exited onto the Ronald Reagan Parkway. I am now totally confused as I believe we are headed in the wrong direction. Again, no one has the nerve to leave our formation. We then exited the Ronald Reagan Parkway onto I-74 south towards Cincinnati. Yes, you are correct. We had simply made a complete circle and we were now headed back to where we started. Since this was one of my first parades, I was afraid to break formation and jeopardize my daughter's volleyball career. Just then, I saw in my rear-view mirror, a parent, no, a Patriot break out of the formation and this parent begins speeding towards the head of the parade. As he passed each car, you could hear the cheers of encouragement coming from the cars of the lost volleyball travelers. He finally reached the head idiot and explained the problem and finally, we were able to reroute our parade.

I have never experienced an act of heroism as I did on that day. This mortal put his daughter's volleyball life on the line to save our ill-fated parade. In the world of club volleyball, you never, ever, challenge the volleyball gods. It is usually better to go in the wrong direction than challenge the lead idiot. I will never forget this Patriot. What is really strange is that this Patriot has never been seen again. A volleyball legend has it that this Patriot was cursed by the volleyball gods for questioning their leadership abilities and was punished to traveling the I-275 loop around Cincinnati for all eternity. Dear brave Patriot, I will never forget you or your sacrifice.

My normal experience with the "Idiots on Parade" strategy is one of terror and fear. Since all the parents anticipate that we are going to "parade" to the tournament, no one bothers to secure directions. It always seems that the lead car is occupied by a Dale Earnhart "wanna-be," and he/she takes off so fast, that most of us are lost ten minutes into our journey. I believe there should be rules for these parades or at least we should take a vote as to who should be the lead idiot. I have also suggested we attach a rope to each car in our parade so we can look as stupid as we feel.

Volleyball Dad Lesson #3
Lead Your Own Parade

I have always urged my daughters to be their own leaders and to always take full accountability for their actions. If my daughters decide to go in the wrong direction, I hope they will quickly find the next exit ramp before bad news finds them. There should be no excuses for making bad decisions. The universal excuse that everyone is now using is, "I just made a mistake, I'm only human." Let me take a moment to clarify what a mistake really is. To me, a mistake is locking your keys in your car or forgetting to bring a book home from school. These oversights are mistakes. If we make a conscious choice to participate in improper behavior, that is not a mistake. That is poor judgment. Poor judgment will result in poor consequences. I believe the following actions are not mistakes: cheating on a test, failure to turn in homework, lying to your parents, not going where you said you were going, hanging with people you were told not to, smoking, drinking, getting into a car with questionable people, attending parties that you know are bad news and drinking *Pepsi* products over *Coke* products. These are not mistakes; these are bad choices that we make. It always frustrates me when someone is caught lying, cheating or stealing. They will always say, "I just made a mistake." I believe we should respond, "No, you did not make a mistake, you voluntarily chose to be an idiot." We should never make it a habit to follow idiots. Lead your own parade. At least then, you will end up at a place of your own choosing. We have created a culture where we feel sorry for someone with bad habits. We should not feel sorry for these individual's, we should feel sorry for the loved ones who are left to pick up the pieces. My two heart attacks have caused my family tremendous pain, and I have no one to blame but myself. Bad habits will always cause bad results. Even Volleyball Dads can hurt the ones they love.

Dad, Do You Believe in Me?

All three of my daughters have participated in the world of volleyball. I sometimes wish they had joined a gang instead. Gangs could not be any more stressful for a parent than club volleyball. I have concluded that after all the yelling, screaming and the tears finally stop, each of my daughters must understand one very critical point – Dad still believes in me. I believe there is a special bond between a Dad and his daughters. I don't believe that Moms can be Dads or that Dads can be Moms. We each bring special skills to our parental responsibilities. If we each do our jobs effectively, a productive member of our society is created.

It is important to remember that when the world seems cruel and our daughters seem to be down on themselves, there must be one constant voice that can be heard through all the noise. That voice belongs to Dads and our never wavering passion to believe in our daughters. Let me ask all the Volleyball Dads a simple question, "Do we believe in our daughters?" Probably a better question is, "Do our daughters *believe* that we believe in them?" Our daughters know if we believe in them or not by simply watching our actions. Our daughters will believe 50% of what we say and 100% of what they see. If our words and actions do not match, our daughters will believe our actions first, then our words.

Our daughters know what is important to us simply by observing where we choose to spend our time. If we never have time to attend their tournaments, we clearly send a signal to our daughters that we value other activities more than watching them compete on the court. If we choose to play golf, they conclude that golf is more important than they are. I believe our daughters will always evaluate the activity we choose and compare that activity to their own self-worth. I never want my daughters to think that cutting the grass is more important than watching them compete in volleyball or life. It is vital that my daughters understand that I will be there to support them anytime and anywhere. Our daughters understand the concept of work commitments, but no matter what they say, they do not understand any *other* activities to be more important than showing our support for their efforts. I am stunned by the number of dads who never attend one of their daughter's volleyball games.

Back in the 1970's, there was a popular song entitled, "The Cats in the Cradle" by Harry Chapin. The song told the story of a Dad who never had time for his child due to his many other commitments. The son was continuously asking the Dad to participate in some activity, but the Dad was always too busy and promised to spend some time with him later. The song ends with the table being turned on the Dad. At the end of the song, the Dad is trying to spend time with his child and the child does not have time to spend with the Dad. The point of the song is simple. The child had grown up to be just like the Dad. The child only had time for himself. I believe my daughters are going to treat me the exact same way that I treated them. If I never had time to support them, they will never find the time to support me.

Volleyball Dads are a special bunch. We understand that our support for our daughters would be nice, but we really know that our support is mandatory. Our children need a solid support system in order to make the proper decisions throughout their lives. Our daughters know that they can always count on Dad to be there to wipe away the tears and to say, "I believe in you" and "I am proud of you." These two statements are the most powerful statements in the world, especially to our daughters. I have always quoted that great philosopher, Frenchy, from the movie *Grease*. At one point in the movie, Sandy was upset and crying over something Danny had done. You know how boys can be. Frenchy gave Sandy this comforting wisdom, "The only guy a girl can depend on is her Daddy." That is our calling and that is our mission in life. I have always believed that everyone needs one special person in their life to pick them up when they fall or to encourage them to pursue their full potential. I believe that it is the responsibility of all Volleyball Dads and dads in general. We *must* answer that call.

Volleyball Dad Lesson #4
Look at Life through Your Daughter's Eyes

I have no way of proving what I am about to say, however, I believe this statement is true. The first thing that all volleyball girls do before their match is canvas the stands to see who is in attendance. I have a habit of watching volleyball players very closely when a match is ready to begin. I watch the eyes of the girls as they look for their parents first and then look to see if any cute boys are in the house. Most girls will never complain, but I believe that deep down they are hoping that Dad will be able to make the match today. They will say they understand, but deep down I don't believe they do. We need to do our best to never let our girls down. We need to make every effort to attend these matches and always support our daughters. I have found that a kind word on a dark day is needed more than we will ever know. I have found this to be true in my business life, as well. As we all know, there are days when we contemplate throwing in the towel. We have had enough and it seems the whole world is stacked up against us. Then it seems that out of nowhere a coworker or a loved one will give you a pat on the back and our whole outlook changes. A few kind words of encouragement can really save the day. I know a few kind words from a loved one can change a life. Our daughters need to occasionally hear a few words of encouragement on their darkest days.

When I was a young boy, I loved to play baseball. My Dad was unable to attend many of my high school baseball games because he drove a delivery truck, and his work schedule would conflict with the games. Before every game, I would scan the stands and look for my Dad; I always hoped that maybe today would be the day that Dad was able to attend. On those rare occasions when Dad was able to attend, I will confess, the game meant more to me than I was willing to admit at the time. I really did try harder and would give 100% on every play, just like Dad would always tell me. My Dad would always say something positive to me after the game. It meant everything to me to play in front of my Dad. No matter what our kids say, having Dad attend their games is a big deal. We may be only one person in this whole-wide world, but to our daughters, we may be the whole-wide world. We must take our responsibilities as Volleyball Dads very seriously. If every Dad in our society would take personal responsibility for their daughters, we would eliminate 90% of chaos that surrounds our daughters. If we are not there for our daughters, they will turn to someone else for guidance. Unfortunately, that someone may not have the best interest of our daughters in mind. Let's stay engaged and raise our own daughters. Sorry for lecturing.

Volleyball Dad Lesson #5
Be There Even When Your Heart is Breaking

I really respect Volleyball Dads who bust their butts to attend their daughter's volleyball matches even though they know their daughter will probably not play a single point. Their daughters are not one of the stars of the team, but they faithfully attend every match in the hope of seeing their daughter compete if only for a few plays. These Dads are the gold-medal Dads. They sit in the stands and pray that maybe tonight will be the night. They send a clear message to their daughters, "I will be there for you in the good times and in the bad times. I will give you unconditional love and support. When you are happy, I am happy. When you are sad, I am sad. Never forget, you will never be alone as long as this Volleyball Dad is on this earth." These words are usually never spoken but are clearly understood between a Dad and his daughter. I have, at times, played this role as several of my daughters would receive limited playing time. Since we love our daughters, watching them sit on the bench is a gut-wrenching experience. But, being true Volleyball Dads, we accept the pain and keep coming back for more. Why? Because that's what Volleyball Dads have done since the beginning of time. We must continue this honorable tradition.

I have always struggled with what to say to my daughters on those bench-warming occasions. The best I could say is, "I'm proud of you." When my daughters laugh and say, "Dad, I didn't even play, why would you be proud of me?" I would then be forced to take the conversation to the next level. I would dig deep into my soul and just speak from the heart. My speech sounded like this, "Volleyball is a great preparer for life. Life can be tough, sometimes real tough. Life will always be unfair. You cannot control what life has planned for you, but you can control how you *react* to life. You sat on that bench and conducted yourself like a team player. You encouraged the chosen ones, and you entered and exited the volleyball court with your head held high. You are a person of class and integrity. This makes you a member of a very small group of people who still occupy this planet. Volleyball is temporary, your dignity is forever. That is why I am proud of you." I would then put my arm around my daughter and we would walk to our car and spend the next fifteen minutes ragging on the coach. This was more for my therapy than my daughter's. Okay, this Volleyball Dad isn't perfect.

Dad, Will Running Make Me a Better Volleyball Server?

For the past thirty years, I have played a very competitive game called "work." Roughly 50% of our population can relate to this concept. I have spent the majority of those thirty years in a leadership role and I have found that the leadership strategies in business and the leadership strategies in volleyball do not share a common approach. I take great pride in studying the art of leadership as my entire career is based on this single skill. Over the years, I have read over five hundred books on leadership and listened to thousands of hours of leadership cassettes. I have studied the leadership strategies of Reagan, Welch, Lincoln and Pitino. I just realized that I have never come across a book about a great volleyball coach. I wonder why?

Several years ago, my daughter Danielle came crawling in the door from a very difficult volleyball practice. Being a compassionate Dad, I asked Danielle what her problem was. Danielle, still grasping for air, explained, "Dad, we all were struggling with our serves today so the coach made us run for most of the practice." Danielle then asked a very profound question, "Dad, will running make me serve better? Shouldn't we spend more time practicing our serving instead of running all the time? I feel like I have signed up for the cross-country team instead of the volleyball team." I pondered Danielle's insight and being a professional leader, I thought about applying this "running" strategy at work.

The next day, I called a meeting with my management team and explained my new leadership strategy. "From now on, whenever a team member makes a mistake, I want that person to run around the building." At first everyone laughed because they naturally assumed I was kidding. I assured the management team I was quite serious. Once they realized I was serious, one of my managers felt compelled to ask, "Why will this help us get better in our business execution?" This manager evidently does not have a daughter playing club volleyball. I explained that in the world of club volleyball, if you want a player to serve well, they are required to run more. I concluded that if this strategy worked in club volleyball, I was sure it would work in our business.

You know what? I just re-read that paragraph and that does sound stupid. It would be like telling our kids to improve their math grades by cutting the grass. The two activities really don't connect in any way. So I began to wonder why this strategy is universally applied in the volleyball world.

After much thought, I came to the following conclusion. The reason Danielle's coaches made the kids run to improve their serving is because *their* coaches made them run when they missed *their* serves. I bet the coach's coaches had to run because *their* coaches made them run for missing a serve. I started to see a trend. This "running-serve" volleyball tradition has been going on for thousands of years. Once a tradition is firmly established, it will take an act of God to change it.

I have also concluded that Adam, *of Adam and Eve fame*, was probably the very first volleyball coach. Here's how I see it. I always believed that there was more to the story of Adam and Eve than just the issue over the apple. I believe the real problem centered on the issue of how many apples Adam and Eve ate while they were in the Garden of Eden. God became upset with them and started yelling, "The score is wrong! You only had one job and that was to simply keep an accurate count of the number of apples you consumed today. Since you obviously can't keep an accurate count, I will punish all mankind because of your negligence." God decided to create a game called volleyball and to add to the frustration of this game, God decided the score would always be wrong. To this day, we are still paying for Adam and Eve's sins.

Here a few other volleyball strategies that I tried to incorporate at work - unsuccessfully I might add.

1. Doing push-ups when a serve is missed. The majority of my work team was unable to get back up once they hit the floor. Some chose to go ahead and sleep while they were down there, instead of sleeping at their desk. I guess the floor was more comfortable.

2. Doing a backward roll when the ball hits the ground, and you lose a point. I chose to ignore this strategy totally. The thought of adults with their butts stuck in the air because they lacked the roll speed to make the backward journey was quite nauseating.

3. Making the team jump up and down during an entire time out. I was never quite sure why this made any sense but I tried it anyway. As the pictures started to

fall off the walls in my conference room and we ran for the defibulator for a few of our team members, I decided to abandon that strategy rather quickly.

Volleyball Dad Lesson #6
Abandon Outdated Traditions

I really try to encourage my daughters to think for themselves. Just because something was done in the past, it does not make it valid today. They must examine the "here and now" and decide what is proper. I do not want them to vote conservative because I do. I want them to fully understand the issues and decide for themselves on how they should vote. If we don't teach our daughters to think, I'm afraid of the people who will begin thinking for them. I believe our daughters, at times, outsource their thinking to the pop culture crowd. They dress just like they are told on television. They listen to absolute crap on the radio. I have noticed that the only times my daughters would listen to this garbage was when they were with other girls in the car. It seems to me that they would turn that channel on because of peer pressure. It was the hip thing to do. The greatest gift that we can share with our daughters is the gift of self-confidence. I encourage my daughters to follow their own judgment. When the day is done, they must live with their own decisions.

One of my favorite stories about thinking involves the exciting world of luggage. Yes, luggage. For thousands of years people have moved around the earth carrying their personal items in bags known as luggage. After thousands of years of our greatest minds participating in this process, it was only recently that some genius said, "Why don't we put wheels on this stuff?" Wow! This genius ignored thousands of years of traditions and was willing to think new thoughts. Today, I'm not sure if you can even buy luggage without wheels anywhere in the world. I want my daughters to look at the world and see new possibilities and new ways to attack a problem. They should never follow the traditions of their coaches if those traditions are illogical. I was excited that my daughter had raised questions about volleyball serving and running. Hopefully, she will be of a new generation of leaders who will look at problem-solving in a whole new light.

Volleyball Dad Lesson #7
Be the Leader of Your Life

Are you a leader or a follower? This single life strategy will determine the course of your life. If my daughters hang with whiners they will become whiners. I urge my daughters to never follow the crowd. As you can tell from reading this book, I am committed to being a sarcastic idiot. I make no apologies for my decision. If you want to determine if you are a leader or a follower, answer these simple questions.

1. If everyone around you decides to lie, cheat and steal, do you participate in order to get along with your friends?

2. If everyone around you decides to attend a P.L.O.M. (poor little old me) party, do you participate or do you simply walk away and find more positive friends to hang with?

3. Do you only do what's right when someone is watching, or do you do the right things because *you* are watching?

4. Do you take total responsibility for your life choices, or do you pray at the altar of victim-hood?

5. Do you hate it when someone you don't know keeps asking you philosophical questions?

Enough! My three daughters are the leaders of their lives. I have never heard one of my daughters say, "Dad, I know that was a dumb thing to do, but everyone else was doing it, so I joined along." I thank God that I never had to begin a lecture by saying, "If everyone decides to be ugly, are you going to be ugly too?"

Princess Di and The W.W.F.

Our society has been warning us about the impact of stress in our daily lives. Study after study has been published linking stress to heart disease, strokes and even cancer. I have observed that everyone responds to stress in different ways and each of us must decide on how to release our stress. I have always contended that everyone has a certain snapping point that will cause them to leave the rational world and enter the world of complete insanity. If you take the most normal person you know and place them under extreme pressure, they will eventually breakdown. I once heard the great motivational speaker, Zig Ziglar, tell a story to illustrate this point. If you take an orange and squeeze it as hard as you can, what do you get? You get orange juice because that is what is *inside* an orange. What do you get when you squeeze a human very hard? You will also get what is *inside*. If you carry around a lot of bad stuff inside, it usually doesn't take much of a squeeze to bring it out.

I suffered two heart attacks at the age of thirty-seven and fifty-one after many years of mismanaging my stress and other related factors. Once the body reaches a certain negative point, it simply will breakdown. Over the past fourteen years I have performed numerous medical stress tests to allow my doctors to monitor my heart condition. If you have ever taken a stress test, you know how intense those ten minutes can be.

I have concluded that a medical stress test is a walk in the park compared to a season of club volleyball. Let's face it - a stress test only takes ten minutes compared to a club volleyball season, which is really a six-month stress test. I believe club volleyball has the ability to bring the worst out in people, even normal people. I'm not even sure how many normal people are actually left anymore, but club volleyball has probably contributed more to our mental heath crisis than any other activity.

The story I am about to share with you may be the most bizarre and unbelievable story ever shared by human beings. I promise you this story is true and the names have not been changed to protect the innocent. In 2003, I witnessed an unthinkable event in my life. My wife, who handles herself with class and refinement, just like Princess Di, clearly lost her mind at the national volleyball tournament in Atlanta. My wife is normally very shy and non-confrontational. I have only heard my wife yell and scream like a maniac when one of my daughters has taken her hairbrush. You simply do not mess with my wife's hair brush.

The volleyball nationals are held at the end of a very long volleyball season. Let me bring you up to date. During one of our matches in Atlanta, the final game of the match concluded with a controversial call going against us. If the point stood, we would lose the match. As the confusion was still taking place on the court, the parents for the next match were hovering around us waiting to pounce on our seats. In the world of club volleyball, once your match is completed, you leave your seats and allow the Romans for the next match to occupy the seats in the coliseum. Since the final call in our match was still in question, we never left our seats. The High Priest was still conferencing with the young Ritalin-deprived kids concerning the last point.

While I was watching the confusion at the scorer's table unfold, a parent from the next match approached me and stated, "Since your team is done, we need your seats." I stated that the final call was in question and we were waiting to see if the match was really over. The parent, or the Vulture as I later called her, was not satisfied with my reply. She persisted, "I don't know why you can't get up and stand behind the seats and wait there so we can sit down." The volleyball stress test had now reached its zenith. I politely yelled, "Back off lady! We will get up when our game is officially over." The more I think about my comments, I realize I was not very polite and was close to a full volleyball meltdown. I finally turned to our parents and using my best sarcastic voice, hollered "We need to all get up because our match must be over because this fat-lady is starting to sing." I believe most of the humans at the tournament, and even several sub-humans, heard my frustration. I left my seat and started to walk away from the Vulture. Did I act like an idiot? Of course I did, but everyone knows I am an idiot, so no one really noticed. What happened next was truly amazing!

Seated next to me during this exchange was my lovely refined and classy wife. Everyone was shocked as Barb reached a full volleyball meltdown. Barb stood up and let this lady have it with both obscene and verbal barrels. Her finger was up in this lady's face and she was using words that would make a sailor blush. The four letters words were flying so fast that I thought I was listening to a rap song. All of our parents were stunned and shocked at what they were observing and hearing. I believe that if there was a puddle of mud available, I would have experienced my first female mud-wrestling event. With God as my witness, I had to pull my wife away from this lady and escort her to a neutral corner. It appeared that the World Wrestling Federation was filming a match right before my very eyes. How many husbands can say they had to separate their wife before she engaged in a fist fight? Once the excitement died down, we finally left the sacred seating area and my wife's blood pressure had dropped to 190 over 150. We decided that the season needed to end quickly before any of us ended up in jail. My wife was starting to have that Charles Manson look in her eyes and I started to worry about my own well-being instead of the Vulture's. At dinner that night, I kept asking the Champ how she felt. I continually stated to Barb that my money was on her the whole time. On our flight home from nationals, I kept a watchful eye on my wife. I would occasionally ask Barb, "Are you hearing the voices now?" We both laughed, as we were relieved that the club volleyball season was finally over. We were happy to be going home and I honestly believe the people in Atlanta were safer once our plane left the ground.

I would highly recommend to everyone who reads this book to comprehend one critical point - *Don't Push Volleyball Parents Too Far*. Everyone has heard of "Road Rage." I'm here to tell you that "Volleyball Rage" is even worse. During the six-month period of a club volleyball season, most parents deal with the chaos pretty well. But at times, the volleyball zealots cross the line. The thought of having a family thrown into a state of confusion for six months is a tough pill for any family to swallow. I believe it would be a benefit to society if all volleyball parents were required by law to hang a sign in their car (usually a van) that said, "Back off! Volleyball parent driving." This would be a public service to all mankind. I think if you look into the background of most mass murderers, you will find that their daughters once played club volleyball. I can't prove this point, but it would explain all the crazy behavior in our society. I may have the translation a bit off, but I believe that Al-Qaeda in English means "Club Volleyball."

Volleyball Dad Lesson #8
Put Life into Proper Perspective

Do we really want to lose emotional energy over a game of volleyball played by young teenage girls? I would say no. I have spent too much time getting caught up in the madness and not realizing how irrelevant volleyball really is. Life is full of *real* problems such as a loved one coping with medical issues or other life altering events. I now follow a very simple life philosophy – *if my family is reasonably happy and healthy, I'm happy*. This strategy allows me to be happy a majority of the time. Life is going to challenge us all. I have found that the key to happiness is to only release my emotional energy under extreme circumstances.

I live twenty-two miles from my office. I must cross the "bridge from hell" everyday from Kentucky to Ohio. At times, I was so affected by the traffic jams that I would roll down my window and scream at the car next to me, "The score is wrong! The score is wrong!" Most people would yell back, "Please don't kill me, you insane volleyball parent." During one of these traffic jam yelling sessions, I had one driver yell back to me, "Get up! We need your seats." I rolled up my window and thanked God that Barb was not in the car. I no longer get upset in traffic, and honestly not much upsets me anymore. Unless someone begins a sentence with the words "the doctor called," I try not to release any emotional energy unless it is a life or death situation.

Dad, the Coach Gave Us the Finger

Over the years, I have had the privilege to observe and play for some of the greatest coaches of all time. I have also read numerous books about the strategies and determination of many of the best coaches in the world. These coaches have inspired me to overcome obstacles in my life and to do my very best to inspire everyone I meet to "pursue their dreams." Great coaches can alter and shape your views on life, work and especially ethics. Unfortunately, very few were in the world of club volleyball. In my humble opinion, I believe most club volleyball coaches are selected directly from the cast of the *Jerry Springer Show*. I know this sounds harsh, as most of the guests on the Springer show are probably not that bad. I don't know any other way to explain behaviors that only

Jerry Springer could appreciate. Let me illustrate for you a real-life example of why I have come to this conclusion.

It was 5:30 a.m. on a Saturday morning. It seems that every volleyball day has 5:30 a.m. as a starting point. Our team met at a local restaurant for our mandatory "Idiots on Parade" march to Columbus, Ohio. This was a huge day in our season. This was our much anticipated Regional Volleyball Tournament. This was the day when each club had the opportunity to prove to the entire region who was number one. Our coach was pumped about the tournament, as she believed we could win the regional title which would lead her to a cover story in the prestigious volleyball magazine, "Volleyball Psycho." The parents were pumped because this was to be our second to last tournament of the season. Everyone's spirits were sky-high for the day, although our motives were quite different.

We finally arrived in Columbus without too much drama and learned that we were to play our first match against the number one team in the region. The team was not only the number one team in our region, but they were one of the top ten teams in the country. After thirty minutes of volleyball action, we were destroyed by the scores of 25-7 and 25-9. In all honesty, the match was not as close as the score indicated. We were beaten so badly that I think our girls wished their mothers were pro-choice fifteen years earlier. It was not pretty. Our coach was visibly upset and sobbing uncontrollably. She really let the girls have it after the match. For the next ten minutes, our girls were scolded for their poor performance and their failure to please the volleyball gods. The parents could only watch as our daughters were verbally destroyed as our coach did her best Bobby Knight imitation. Being a Volleyball Dad, I have always found these moments to be the most challenging. My daughter was suffering and there was nothing I could do because a parent intervention is a criminal offense in the world of club volleyball. If a parent challenges the sanity of the coach, the parent may ruin their daughter's chance of ever playing in a volleyball game in this life and probably their next life too.

Our girls were really upset after the coach's lecture, and almost all the girls were now sobbing uncontrollably. The parents were still on their natural high, as this was the second to last tournament of the season. As we were standing on the sidelines and watching this drama unfold, the parents were now concerned because it was unusual to have so many people crying by 8:30 a.m. It is not unusual to have a couple of girls crying, but to have the majority of the girls in tears was particularly alarming. As I looked on from the parent's penalty box (we are never allowed too get to close to the girls), I notice that our coach was really doing a tsunami rain dance from both eyes. Her mascara was dripping down her face. With her long black hair and the black dripping mascara, she looked like the old-time rocker Alice Cooper. For those of you who are under forty years of age, Alice Cooper is a guy. I even thought I saw a python wrapped around her neck. (Alice Cooper would wrap a python around his neck during his concerts.) I quickly realized that it was not a python; it was just me with my hands mentally wrapped around her neck. You see, in the world of club volleyball, it is very difficult to tell the difference between the real and the unreal. I eventually started to laugh and thought about how much fun the next twelve hours were going to be.

When the coach was done screaming at the girls, she instructed them to go out in the hall and have a team meeting to discuss their awful performance. She also instructed the girls to *not* stop and talk with their parents. As you are starting to learn, somehow the parents are a negative force in the eyes of volleyball coaches. I don't pretend to understand this belief, I just continue to witness every volleyball coach repeat this statement. After the team broke their huddle, my daughter immediately walked over to me and rolled her eyes and said, "Dad, I'm not allowed to talk to you." I asked her if her mother told her that again, in a joking manner, and she quickly advised me that it was a directive from the coach. I told her to follow the coach's orders, but to keep me informed of what I was not supposed to know. She agreed and entered the secret meeting of the volleyball sisterhood.

Shortly after the meeting started, several of our girls were spotted running to the restroom crying as if they just found out that Bambi died. The parents then called a parent meeting to discuss what we should do. Should we go after our girls and console them or should we go to breakfast. After a short discussion, I decided to order a cheese omelet and a Diet Coke. I know this may sound cruel, but after ten years of observing the world of volleyball, I've discovered that girls' crying during a tournament is as common as the score being wrong. The parents began to hunker down for a long hard emotional tournament.

I should have known that this was going to be tough day. During our match, our girls received the "finger" on two separate occasions from our coach. One of the worst things that could happen to our girls was to receive the "finger" during a match. Let me explain what I mean. When our girls are playing bad, our coach would call a timeout. As the team approached the bench looking for encouragement or direction, the coach would not standup. She would simply point her finger to end of the bench. That was her way of saying, "Go talk among yourselves, I'm too disgusted with you to even leave my chair and scream at you." The girls would then mope down to the end of the bench and probably talk about their weekend plans or their boyfriends. Finally, the High Priest would blow his/her whistle to signal the end of the timeout, and our girls would return to the court without ever talking to the coach. On this particular morning, the coach had given our girls the "finger" twice before 8:30 a.m. Our coach's behavior really upset me, but my wife reminded me that this was our second last tournament and a slight feeling of euphoria filled my senses. The season was almost over.

Volleyball Dad Lesson # 9
Leaders Need to Lead.

As a Volleyball Dad, I know I need to coach my daughters on the good days and the bad days. It's easy to be a great coach when everything is going well. However, a coach is really needed when things are going bad. Our daughters need our guidance on their darkest and most challenging days. I have seen my share of fair-weather coaches during my life and I have come to respect the coaches who are there when the times are tough. I have witnessed many coaches laugh and have a good-old time when the team is winning, but as soon as the team starts losing, a total personality change occurs. Coach Normal can quickly transform to Coach Abnormal. I believe the players are looking for consistency by the coach, not a strategy similar to a roller-coaster ride. My best advice to any leader is to be consistent. A leader's approach to the game should not change by the scoreboard. I have learned in my leadership career that people want a steady hand at the wheel. People prefer someone who never gets too high and never gets too low. I try to teach my daughters that coaches and friends are much the same. Both will be there for you during the good times, but only a few will be there when you really need them. I hope my daughters cherish their good coaches, as well as their good friends. Great coaches and great friends belong to a small sorority.

Volleyball Dad Lesson # 10
Leaders Inspire People.

Have you ever spent ten minutes with someone and you feel a surge of "can-doism" after you walk away? Someone who can leave you in a better place than they found you, is simply a great leader. After I listen to motivational speaker Zig Ziglar, I feel better about my future. I believe volleyball has taught my daughters to recognize great leaders in life. Some coaches earn the respect of their players and many coaches earn the respect of no one. I hope my daughters learn a few valuable life lessons and hopefully, even find an excellent role model along the way. If a coach decides to take an ego trip, they usually find that they will travel alone. I believe our daughters want a tough and inspirational coach. Our girls want someone who will push them to reach their full potential. Most of us, if left to our own devices, would never use our God-given athletic talents. Why? Because we are normally lazy, and we hope and pray someone will come along and inspire us to "go for it." Great coaches will inspire our daughters to pursue excellence and poor coaches will inspire our daughters to appreciate the great coaches. Great coaches, just like great leaders, will take us places that we never knew we could reach.

When I was growing up in Kentucky, I had two great coaches in my life. I was fortunate to be able to call them Mom and Dad. No matter how bad I played, or the outcome of the game, my parents always made me feel that tomorrow was going to be a better day. My Dad would always give me advice on how to improve my skills and Mom would always just say, "I think you are the best player on the team." I know her statement was not accurate, but when my Mom looked me in the eyes and said that, I really believed that she believed it. Even though I knew it was not true, it did provide comfort on those difficult sporting days. The idea of unconditional love and support by parents is critical to any young athlete. Mom and Dad are the most powerful coaches in our children's lives. Let's use our power for good, not evil.

In my professional career, I have taught a self-development course to our employees entitled, "The Eagle Leadership Program." When I ask adults at work to tell me who their heroes in life are, they always start talking about their parents. Mom and Dad are the center of the universe for so many people, and I don't believe all Moms and Dads understand this fact. Our daughters and sons look to Mom and Dad for approval at all times. I don't care if you are nine years old or fifty-two years old, it is very important to us to make sure Mom and Dad are proud. I constantly tell my girls that I am proud of them. I don't believe anyone ever gets tired of hearing those words.

Volleyball Dad Lesson # 11
The Finger Strategy Doesn't Work.

Since I am always looking for new and effective leadership strategies, I attempted to use the "finger strategy" at the office. One day I called a meeting with my management team to review our latest performance results. The results were lousy in all areas of our operations. I decided I had nothing to lose, so I gave the "finger strategy" a try with my management team. I arrived early for our standard Friday morning meeting and took a seat at the far end of the conference room. When the management team arrived, I never looked up. I simply pointed my finger towards the opposite corner of the conference room. My team stopped and stared at me as they were obviously confused by my bizarre behavior. As I continued to point my finger to the opposite corner, one member of my team stated, "You're right Tom, we are number one." I looked up and shook my head in the negative and continued to point to the opposite corner. My team just didn't understand my new leadership strategy. After several tries, I just gave up and told my team to take their seats. As they settled into their chairs, one of my team members asked, "Tom, what the hell were you doing? I thought you were warning us that a mass murderer was behind the door! Tom, are you okay?" I confessed to the team that I was at a volleyball tournament all weekend and I was just trying out some new leadership techniques. My team pleaded with me to stop attending my daughter's volleyball tournaments, as they had to deal with my bizarre behavior every time I returned. They even offered to place a couch in the conference room so I could lie down for a while. I was starting to realize that these amazing volleyball coaching techniques were not transferable to the world of business.

I must confess. I have never understood how the coaches evaluate the players on their teams. I have witnessed my daughter start a game and proceed to play the game of her life. During the game, she was nothing short of a volleyball diva. Then, the next game, she sits on the bench and never plays a single point. I just don't understand the logic, or should I say the lack of logic. I once heard a motivational speaker, Tony Robbins, tell a story that helped me understand why this strange behavior occurs on a regular basis.

There was a frog and a scorpion standing on the side of a river. Both were trying to figure out a way to cross the river. Finally, the scorpion says to the frog, "Let me jump on your back so I can safely cross the river." The frog replied, "Are you nuts? Scorpions sting and kill frogs. Why in the world would I let you kill me?" The scorpion became frustrated with the frog's attitude and the frog's failure to understand the obvious. The scorpion explained the frog's faulty logic, "If I sting you while we are crossing the river," the scorpion said, "not only will you die, but I will drown in the process. Your logic doesn't make sense. Why would I want to kill myself?" The frog thought about the scorpion's point and concluded that the scorpion was correct. The frog told the scorpion to jump on his back, and they began to make their way across the river. As they were halfway across the river, the scorpion stung the frog in the back of the neck. As the frog was going down for the final count, he looked at the scorpion and said, "You idiot, what have you done. Not only am I going to die, you are going to die, too. Why did you sting me?" The scorpion simply stated, "I'm a scorpion and scorpions sting frogs. That's what we do."

This story has helped me understand bizarre behavior in the world of volleyball and the world of life. I have concluded that you cannot follow the logic of the volleyball gods. You must simply understand, "That's what volleyball coaches do." Just like the scorpion, the behavior does not make sense to the logical part of our society, but to scorpions and volleyball coaches – it's just what they were born to do.

Since I am a glutton for punishment, I decided to try this strategy of benching my high performers in the business world. I called our top salesperson into my office one Monday morning, and I commended him on his excellent performance during the previous week. I then informed him that I did not want him to "play" in the upcoming sales week. He looked confused as to why I chose to bench him after such an excellent week. I explained to him that I just returned from my daughter's volleyball tournament, and I was trying out a few new coaching techniques that I learned from my daughter's coaches. The salesman smiled and asked me if I was still hearing the volleyball voices in my head. When I replied, "Yes, the voices are very loud today," he suggested I lay down for awhile, and he proceeded to call the company nurse. While I was still horizontal and attempting to find Planet Earth in my head, I kept yelling out, "The score is wrong! The score is wrong!" The nurse quickly rushed in and sedated me. I really need to quit trying volleyball coaching techniques at the office.

Volleyball Suicide Hotline,
"I'm Sorry, All Lines are Busy."

My first exposure to club volleyball occurred in 1995. Prior to this date, I never knew this dark world even existed. To this day, I refer to it as the "volleyball cult world." Here's how it all started. My wife received a telephone call from my daughter's grade school volleyball coach advising us that a gentleman was going to start a new club. If we were interested, we needed to contact this gentleman as soon as possible. His name was not initially revealed. I secretly referred to him as "Mr. Gentleman." Since my daughter had not been selected during another recent club volleyball tryout, we decided to check out this new club.

We attended the meeting and learned about the exciting world of club volleyball. We were informed that there would be several practices per week, at a yet to be determined secret location. The tournament schedule was brutal. I thought my daughter was trying out for the NBA. It seemed that a tournament was scheduled every weekend from February to June of 1995. I felt like I was involved in a witness protection program that required me to travel from one secret location to another.

There were no tryouts, and the first ten people to write the required checks were to be on the team. Since we felt we had no other options, we wrote the check and waited for our new secret society adventure to begin. I honestly expected to receive a call in the middle of the night instructing me to visit a telephone booth in some isolated location and wait to receive my new instructions. The whole experience was odd and seemed very secretive.

Our team started out with three coaches. I was impressed that a team of ten twelve-year-old girls who wanted to play volleyball required three coaches. I didn't know if my daughter was gifted or was so bad that three coaches were needed to compensate for her lack of talent. Shortly after the initial practice, our coaching staff was down to two coaches for some unknown reason. As the season progressed, our coaching staff disappeared quicker than Rosie O'Donnell attacking a box of Krispy Cream doughnuts. It really started to get strange when our two remaining coaches had a disagreement with the club's

General Manager. One of the exiled coaches called our house one evening and advised me that the club General Manager was taping his telephone calls with the parents and she was contacting us to alert us of this strange behavior. The parents were now in the full conspiracy mode, and our telephone was ringing off the hook. One night, I actually answered the telephone, "Volleyball suicide hotline – all lines are busy." On the other end of the telephone was one of our exiled coaches. She seemed stunned by my odd behavior, but she still went on and relayed more bizarre information. Please remember, this chaos is circulating around my seventh grade daughter's volleyball team. I told the coach that I could not talk to her until I enacted the "cone of silence." (This phrase was popular in the television series *Get Smart* in the 1960's and yes, it was the "cone of silence".) I think the exiled coach started to believe that I was more bizarre than our General Manager. While I found the whole experience entertaining, I quickly learned that this drama was very serious to many volleyball parents. I mentioned this madness to another volleyball parent who just smiled and said, "Welcome to the world of club volleyball." I started to learn that this drama is the norm, not the exception.

Our team had now lost three coaches. We were able to find a fourth and temporary coach to help us through the tournament for the upcoming weekend and finally we were then able to secure our *fifth* coach of the season. Keep in mind, the club volleyball season is only six-months long. I believe McDonald's has less turnover than our coaching staff did during our first club volleyball season.

Volleyball Dad Lesson # 12
Dysfunctional Kids Come From Dysfunctional Parents

There are many adults who I consider to be unstable, at best. I understand that many people believe I am a bit odd as well. That's America. I believe that the pressure we as parents put on our kids is dangerous. I have always believed that punks probably have punks for parents. A kid that displayed a lack of respect for authority probably grew up in a family that disrespected authority. All of us simply reflect the environment we grew up in. My Dad had very poor eating habits. I have very bad eating habits. I have now learned that eating bacon at every meal was probably not a heart-healthy choice. My Dad was overweight. I am overweight. My Dad loved statistics. I love statistics. I know I am not breaking new ground here, but 80% of the time our kids will grow up and be just like us. It will take a lot of determination to break this tradition, but it can be done. I encourage my kids to take the best I have to offer and discount the rest. I am very confident that our daughters are not going to make their careers or find their place in this world based on volleyball. I have always hoped it would be a good competitive learning experience, not a scene out of *One Flew Over The Cuckoo's Nest*. I believe that if we want our girls to be crazy, then club volleyball is probably an excellent option.

I'm sure everyone has witnessed at least one example of a parent losing their mind at a volleyball tournament. I even know parents who were thrown out of a volleyball match for some ugly behavior. Most kids will imitate their parents. Many kids will display excellent manners and many kids will be absent of all manners. I must confess, I am a very sarcastic person with a very competitive nature. This is probably not a very good combination when you add a little frustration to the formula. I constantly instruct my kids to back off the sarcasms as they could cause a few problems. As an example, I have made the following regrettable comments during a volleyball match:

"These line judges must be Stevie Wonder's kids."

"If you look up idiot in the dictionary, I bet you will find a picture of that coach."

"I bet Donald Trump dreams about firing that coach."

"I believe club volleyball is really a mental disorder."

"My heart attacks were more enjoyable than this tournament."

"Girls, never make fun of people unless you are absolutely sure you can get away with it."

"Wow! That girl is huge, let's call her Shrek."

"It's not important if you win or lose, what's important is where you place the blame."

"These parents are *almost* as obnoxious as we are."

While I may find my humor entertaining for the moment, I know I am setting a bad example for my daughters. Unfortunately, all of my daughters have picked up on my sarcasms and they can turn a wise-crack with the best of them. I am constantly lecturing my girls to not act like their Dad. I know the negative influence I am having on my girls and I do try to minimize my humor. I'm never quite sure how to respond when someone says to me, "Tom, your daughters are just like you." I'm not sure if I should say, "Thank you" or "I'm sorry."

Volleyball Dad Lesson # 13
Develop a Winning Effort Mentality.

I have a saying that I constantly share with my daughters, "Winning isn't everything, but the effort to win is." I believe this statement is true in all areas of our lives. The amount of effort my daughters put forth in pursuing their dreams is more important than the final score. If we put forth a maximum effort in everything we do, the final score will take care of itself. Life can be unpredictable. However, our level of effort in our daily lives should always be predictable. Pursuing excellence is simply a learned habit that is no different than learning to ride a bike. If we do not commit to excellence in all areas of our lives, we will develop poor habits which will lead to future problems. I don't care if my daughters are just baking cookies. I encourage them to make the best cookies in the history of baking cookies. Good habits equal good results.

Let me extend a challenge to all Volleyball Dads. Tomorrow, when you go to work, I want you to really elevate your passion and commitment to excellence at the office. I want you to really go for it for eight hours, as if your job is on the line. At the end of the day, see if anyone at work notices your new level of passion and see if you feel different about your level of performance. I bet both your coworkers and you will see you in a new light. Please write this phrase on your forehead – *"Pursue excellence and opportunity will pursue you."* I not only say that phrase to my daughters, I usually say that phrase as I arrive at the office. I know that if I don't set the proper example for my daughters, I will be sending mixed signals to them. If Dad does not approach his job with passion and commitment, why should I!

Minutemen And Volleyball Parents

One of my favorite hobbies is reading about the American Revolutionary War. I have always been inspired by our history and I have learned numerous lessons by studying the brave Americans who have shaped this nation. History has captured the heroic stories of the Minutemen. During the Revolutionary War, these brave patriots were ready to fight in a moment's notice. These warriors of freedom were prepared to drop everything they were doing and take up arms to defend the cause of freedom. The Minutemen believed that "fighting the cause" was their calling in life, and they were prepared to give their lives to defend the cause of freedom.

Being a volleyball parent is pretty much the same thing. I have come to realize that the lives of the Minutemen and the lives of volleyball families are quite similar. It is not unusual for my daughter to receive a telephone call informing her that a practice session has been scheduled in the next two hours. In the world of club volleyball, every hour could lead you in a different direction. I believe the earliest cases of A.D.D. were found in the world of club volleyball. Everything is a last second ordeal in the realm of club volleyball.

During a club volleyball season, the ringing of the telephone is a traumatic event. The entire family holds its collective breaths as if a secret mission is about to be revealed. If the telephone call is from the secret volleyball underworld, my family must quickly begin evaluating the message. Once the secret volleyball message is decoded, our family mobilizes into action. On this particular night, a secret volleyball practice had been scheduled. We immediately canceled all plans for the evening. Dinner plans are cancelled or the frozen food is returned to the non-volleyball section of our freezer. The telephone networking begins. We may be required to drive to practice or pickup from practice. However, this critical information is never determined until seconds before the event is to take place. My family operates in a lockdown mode until the event is properly planned. Volleyball parents must learn to excel in the art of time management. Events will change so quickly, you must be able to adapt or risk having a FVM (full volleyball meltdown.) If you have never witnessed a parent experiencing a FVM, trust me, it is not a pretty sight.

Once the decoded message is verified to be authentic, my family is focused on executing the mission. I then instruct my older daughters to monitor the police scanner to see if there are any major traffic jams that would delay our planned travel route, and we immediately search the weather channels for evidence of any possible weather delays. As many volleyball parents know, our daughters need to arrive at least thirty minutes before the scheduled practice time in order to properly warm-up. A late arrival may cause a major crisis in the volleyball world, as well as creating emotional harm to my family. Our entire family changes on a dime to serve the cause of volleyball. Just like the Minutemen, we are dedicated warriors for the cause of volleyball. I pray we have served in an acceptable manner.

Being a typical Dad, I like to try and play golf on the weekends. However, being a Volleyball Dad, this can become quite a challenge. On several occasions, we have learned on Thursday or Friday that we have a tournament or scrimmage scheduled for Saturday. How do you wake up on Thursday or Friday and decide to have a volleyball tournament on Saturday? I will never understand the mental wiring that makes up the volleyball mind. Regardless, securing additional details is simply impossible. I normally start to ask several basic questions. Is it an all day tournament? How many teams are in the tournament? Should we pack a volleyball survival kit? After the third, "Dad, I don't know." I just stop asking questions. I cancel my golf plans and call a family meeting to deal with the crisis. I locate my revolutionary Brown Bess musket and prepare to report for duty.

Volleyball Dad Lesson # 14
Be Flexible or Take Blood Pressure Medicine.

In the business world, popular culture teaches us to accept change immediately. I feel very confident that when the world of business describes "change," it has no idea what change really is. I would like to see the CEOs of Fortune 500 Companies manage the changes that take place in a typical club volleyball season, or for that matter, in a typical one-day volleyball tournament. I have witnessed the actual location of the tournament change on the day of the tournament. In Ken Blanchard's popular book, "Who Moved My Cheese," we are taught to accept change or we risk being left behind. The world is a hectic and messy place and life does change without warning. The world of club volleyball has taught me the meaning of change – accept instant change or accept a life of mental disorder. If you learn to accept instant change, you will find an inner peace. One of the hidden benefits of club volleyball is the reality of constant change.

This crazy culture does condition you to "roll with the punches." John Lennon probably said it best, "Life is what happens to you while you're busy making other plans." I wonder if John Lennon had a daughter who played club volleyball?

Volleyball Dad Lesson # 15
Don't Answer the Telephone.

I have often wondered what would happen if we took all of our telephones out of our homes. I know this sounds bizarre. Everyone today believes that instant communication is required at all times. It seems we have all become doctors overnight and need to secure life-threatening information immediately. Think about the no telephone strategy for just a minute and how that single strategy would change the quality of our lives. My kids would probably go into "telephone withdrawal syndrome." There would be no interruptions or last minute crisis-calls. The world of gossip would come to a complete halt, as most of us are too lazy to actually visit someone's home to discuss these petty issues. The invention of the telephone has caused the act of gossip to travel at the speed of light. I guess as a society, we love interruptions so much that we now carry cell phones, pagers and other gadgets with us 24/7. I believe we have created our own Minutemen culture by embracing instant communication. I really like the "no telephone" rule in the home. If something is important, someone will drive over and tell me in person. How many volleyball telephone calls in your home begin with the phrase, "Did you hear?" When the conversation begins with those three little words, I know my wife will be tied up for the next hour, at least. Remember that instant communication can lead to instant insanity.

How Many Flowers Did Your Daughter Have?

For many years, I have preached that the Dudley-Do-Rights (DDRs) in our society will destroy our world. They are so concerned about "everyone's" well-being that they have decided to run our lives for us. They make us wear seat belts. They try to control our eating habits, and they even tell us how we need to throw away our garbage. Thank God these DDR's are saving us from us. I honestly believe that the DDRs will require us to wear a helmet when we drive our cars someday. I have a vision of a DDR on national television crying and defending this insanity by passionately whining, "If we can reduce just one head injury, isn't this new law worth it?" Of course, the correct answer that you will never hear is, "No! Go away you intruding little control freak and let me live my life on my own terms, not yours." The DDRs in our society are constantly lecturing us about how to raise our kids. They are the geniuses who are self-appointed masters in the proper way to feed our kids, what television shows our kids should watch, what movies our kids should watch, and what books our kids are allowed to read. They are the self-proclaimed experts on how we are to communicate with our kids. They usually start out every sentence with, "If we can save just one child…" The DDRs believe the "one child" phrase gives them the moral high ground to try and run our lives.

I recently read an article in the newspaper that a bunch of DDRs are trying to outlaw "chatter" from little league baseball. The proud tradition of baseball chatter – "swing batter swing," "this guy can't hit," "everyone move in" – will soon be outlawed from baseball. The DDRs are starting to go from annoying to down right dangerous. I fear they are robbing our society of a much needed characteristic – mental toughness. They insist on turning everyone into a whiner-victim who is filled with emotional scars from the big bad world. If our children are to survive in this world, mental toughness must be part of their foundation.

I keep waiting for the DDRs to attack the world of volleyball. The DDRs are responsible for refusing to grade papers in our schools with red pens because it makes the student *feel* bad. I have always found that the number written on my test scores was more upsetting than the color of the inked involved, but these people are the self-proclaimed geniuses on our feelings.

Sorry, DDRs infuriate me. Let's get back to our important discussion on volleyball. There is a phrase now used in the world of volleyball when one parent talks to another parent after a game. It normally sounds like this, "How many kills did your daughter have in that match?" Let me explain what a "kill" is in the world of volleyball. Once a player sends a pass to the setter, the setter then sets the ball for the hitters. If the hitter pounds the ball to the ground and receives a point, the effective hit is scored as a "kill." When keeping score in volleyball, the statistician records the number of kills each player has. If you read the volleyball scores in the newspaper, you will see the number of kills clearly on display. How long do you think it is going to be before a DDR wants to change this "violent" term to something like "flowers?" I can hear them now.

The DDRs would passionately state, "Look at what we are teaching our young daughters. We are sending a message that killing is good and that you can be a star if you could learn how to kill more. We need to teach love and understanding, not hate and murder. In order to begin the healing process, I believe we should change this evil word from "kills" to "flowers." I believe that world peace could be achieved if we make this change now. Remember the lyrics in this famous song, "*Let There be Peace on Earth and Let it Begin with Me.*" Just for those of you keeping score at home, that song did not bring about any peace.

Quit laughing! You know this event is coming. I just hope I am present when they make their compassionate speech. I believe I will probably respond, "Ms. DDR, please do not take my comments the wrong way, but I think you are certifiably nuts!" I would then quit being nice and say, "Why should we stop there, let's make the following changes as well:

- Let's change the word "match" to "gathering." The word "match" just sounds too competitive. It sends a message that there will be winners and losers and that reality is just not compassionate. The DDR's goal is to make sure our kids are slaughtered when they reach the real adult world and their only hope will be for the government, or should I say DDRs, to take care of them. "Match," also strikes up an image of fires and fires can kill people. Therefore, using the word "match" is actually encouraging volleyball girls to kill people. Once this link is endorsed by the DDRs, protest marches outside of volleyball tournaments cannot be far behind.

- Let's change the word "serve" to "kisses." Serve sounds so subservient and really wouldn't the world be a better place if we would send more "kisses" to each other. Again, the word "serving" implies a master-slave relationship. This is America! No one should have to serve someone else.

- Let's change the word "block" to "returning love." The word "block" is so negative and creates an image that we are establishing barriers between each other. These barriers cause a breakdown in communication and that can lead to hurt feelings. That can't be good. This change would allow the players to stay connected in a new emotional and positive way. This bond could eliminate the need for future wars. If we eliminate future wars, we will not need future peace songs and peace marches. I believe we all agree - *that would be a good thing*.

- Let's change the word "dig" to "uplifting flowers." When a volleyball player goes low and is able to pass the ball after a hit, it is commonly said to be a great "dig."

The word dig reminds us of gravediggers and that can't be positive. What kind a message would this send to our kids? Subliminally, we are forcing our kids to think about death and grave-digging. When will this madness stop! If we change the phrase to "uplifting flowers," doesn't that create more love in the world? If we change "kills" to "flowers" then was must change "digs" to "uplifting flowers." They just go together.

You get the idea. I completely understand the concept of using words to motivate or inspire people. However, the idea of changing words to promote love and harmony will not create love and harmony. I am very pleased that the "word police" have not found their way to the volleyball world. I will predict that these words will change, as soon as more people from our educational system become volleyball coaches.

Volleyball Dad Lesson # 16
Our Beliefs Will Shape Our Lives, Not Our Words.

If our daughters believe in the wrong words, they will be choosing the wrong world to live in. If they believe they are ugly, they will be ugly. If they believe they are dumb, they will be dumb. The words are only a symptom of the problem. The real problem is what our girls *really* think of themselves. Let's face it. The world can be a tough and cruel place for our daughters. There must be one voice and one place where our daughters can hear and believe – "You are beautiful. You are a great kid. If your friends are mean, don't change, just find new friends. If your teachers and coaches are nasty, ignore them. These people are just like an upset stomach, take some Maalox and wait for them to pass."

My point here is very important. I want my daughters to believe in themselves and not live their life trying to please everyone around them. I believe you cannot make miserable people happy, so don't even try. Some people are not happy unless they are unhappy. Ignore these fools and don't take the bait and never attend their pity parties. Remember, when you dance with the devil, the devil doesn't change, you do. As Volleyball Dads, we must keep our daughters away from the prophets of doom. This is a very difficult but necessary job.

What we *think* of ourselves is everything. If other people think nice things about us, that is great, but it is not mandatory. I think this story will illustrate my point. Let's say I'm back in high school and my only mission in life is to ask girls out on dates. I spot a major babe named Barb standing in front of me at McDonalds. I tell my buddies that I'm going to ask her out on date. I tap this fox on the shoulder and say, "Hi, my name is Tom, would you like to go out on a date with me?" Barb takes a minute, checks me out and says, "No, thank you. I need to stay home tonight and count my socks." Shot down cold. All my buds are laughing and asking me how it felt to be humiliated in front of everyone? As I walked away from that apparent disaster, I had a choice to make. Do I listen to my inner-voice number one or my inner-voice number two?

Inner-voice number one will shout, "You idiot. I can't believe you asked that girl out. She is way out of your league. You're fat, ugly, stupid and you only have three teeth. Why would anyone want to go on a date with you? Look at everyone laughing at you! You need to crawl in a hole and hide for the rest of your life."

Or, you could listen to voice number two, "I'm proud of you. That took a lot of guts to ask that girl out. You could have made a better presentation but now you have something to work on. If you keep developing a *go for it* mentality, there is nothing you can't do in life. Hang in there. You are on the right path. I'm proud to be the voice in your head. You might also want to look into getting some dentures. Your teeth look pretty nasty from in here." Which voice do most of us listen to? Unfortunately, the usual winner is voice number one. Voice number one promotes rejection and voice number two promotes hope. Which voice will each of us listen to? If the DDRs have their way, no one will need to learn how to manage rejection since no one will ever feel the pain of rejection.

I believe that words are important but they are not nearly as important as the voices we hear in our head every day. If we listen to the right voice, the words spoken by someone else will never matter to us. Someone once asked me this question, "If everyone has these two voices in their head, one that is negative and one that is positive, which voice will eventually win in the end?" A great question deserves a great answer. I explained, "The inner-voice that will win in the end, is always the inner-voice that we choose to feed every day." If we feed the "can-do" inner-voice, we will see the world as full of opportunities. If we feed the "can't-do" inner-voice, we will see ourselves as a victim in a hopeless and very depressing world. We are simply what we eat.

Will Work for Food, My Daughter Plays Club Volleyball

I have often wondered if the majority of the homeless people in America or those begging for money on the street corners were once involved in the club volleyball cult. I am sure I recognized a homeless man recently at one of our volleyball tournaments, and after I placed two pennies in his tin cup (yes, I am quite a compassionate person), I heard him yell out, "The score is wrong! The score is wrong!" Since that day, I have prayed that he has sought professional help or, at least, joined the local chapter of V.A. (Volleyball Anonymous).

The parents involved in club volleyball spend money faster than the federal government and that is not easy to do. The amount of money we fork out in the name of volleyball is astounding. This past season our volleyball team, located in Northern Kentucky, participated in tournaments in Kansas City, Chicago (twice), Tampa, Houston and Columbus, Ohio. I was quite pleased that our tournament on Mars was canceled because they could not find enough water to "sell" us during the tournament. I'm still stunned that we buy water when water is free. At the time of this writing, a gallon of gasoline is close to $3 per gallon. Compared to 12 ounces of water, gasoline seems to be a real bargain. I have encouraged my daughters to start drinking gasoline instead of water, it's much cheaper. Our coaches always require our girls to drink water at all tournaments. I've often wondered how many coaches work at Water-R-Us.

On a side note, I have never understood why water is the official drink in the world of volleyball. My daughter, Danielle, hates drinking water. I'm embarrassed to admit this. During one of Danielle's tournaments, I took her water bottle to a secure location and emptied out the water and replaced the water with a Coke. *Yes, a carbonated drink.* I felt like I was assisting an alcoholic and actually thought of having my attorney on stand by, just in case the volleyball secret police figured out our scam. Be honest, I'm sure you have done similar antics.

At a recent tournament, it was my job to run and buy the mandatory water during a timeout. I hustled to the concession stand and yelled, "I need a bottle of water." The concession cashier, let's call her "Lightning," shuffled to the cooler in slow-motion to obtain the water. When she finally arrived back at the counter, I reintroduced myself as the gentleman who was in a hurry. She "quickly" rang up my order and said, "That will be $3.50." I must have looked confused, or she thought I was hard-of-hearing, as she repeated the amount in a very loud voice. I replied, "Ma'am, I ordered one bottle of water, not Lake Erie." Even though I thought it was a funny line, "Lightning" was not amused or she had no idea that Lake Erie is a large body of water. I gave her the shirt off my back and headed back to the court.

Many of these tournaments require airline travel and living in the Cincinnati area, this is not a cheap method of transportation. Since Cincinnati is a major hub for Delta, it is a major pain in the butt to fly out of Cincinnati to anywhere. The majority of our volleyball parents will drive or walk to Louisville, Lexington, Dayton or Columbus to obtain cheaper airfares. If you choose to fly out of Cincinnati, you better bring the big wallet with you as airfare could be as much as $1000 per ticket. Remember that these are *teenage* girls, not a major college football team. Our volleyball team does not have boosters or alumni who we can count on to offset some of our costs. We must do it the old-fashion American way – we must pay our own bills. Doesn't that sound like a strange concept in America today?

I estimate that our family spent $7,000 during the past club volleyball season. I will confess that some of that money was spent on therapy for me, as I sometimes didn't deal with the chaos very well. Over the past ten years, we have spent in excess of $40,000 on volleyball related expenses. I know many parents will say, "Hey, maybe she will receive a scholarship." I usually respond that maybe my daughters could study to become a psychiatrist and find a cure for this nasty volleyball disease. I think a volleyball scholarship would allow us to breakeven at this point. When I was a kid, I think our parents would spend maybe $25 per year for us to play on our baseball and basketball teams. There were no overnights, no $100 shoes every year and no fees required. Man, has the world changed!

Let me ask the obvious question. Is the money we spend on club volleyball worth it? Of course, the answer is yes. The world of club volleyball does an excellent job of preparing our girls for the real world. Let's face it; the real world is even crazier than the world of club volleyball. Our girls will learn that not only is life not fair, they will learn that crazy people are in charge of many of our businesses, universities and government institutions. The world of club volleyball will allow our girls to experience a brief view into the world of business and the idiots that operate them. Incompetent leaders are everywhere in the world. God must really love incompetent people because He made an endless supply of them.

This next story is one of my favorites and helps relate how surreal the volleyball world is about spending money. We were playing in a tournament in Kansas City, and as we were preparing to check-out of our hotel, I received a frantic message from a volleyball messenger. The messenger stated that I should not check out of our room. I was informed that the coach needed to have one room available for her once she returned from watching her daughter's matches. Our coach's daughter was not on our team but was playing at the same tournament. The coach wanted to return to the hotel later that afternoon with her daughter and needed a room to shower and to sacrifice a chicken to the volleyball gods. I decided to decline her order and I placed my daughter's volleyball career in jeopardy. I was not prepared to be charged for an extra day at the hotel for our coach's hygiene needs. I must confess that I knew our coach needed a room, but my hotel room did not have padded walls. I guess, in her eyes, wasting $100 on a shower room was not a big deal, especially since we had already handed over thousands of dollars.

Please! Contact My Agent

It's November, you can start to feel the excitement of the upcoming club volleyball season. Parents begin making volleyball to-do lists, such as refilling blood pressure and Prozac prescriptions. The girls are all full of anticipation. It's the season for volleyball tryouts. November is a special month in the world of club volleyball. This is the month when all the local teams conduct their much anticipated team tryouts and it finally brings an end to the months of lobbying and political maneuvering by parents and players. I once heard someone involved in the world of volleyball state that "Politics is not involved in the team selection process." After hearing this statement, most parents politely smile and silently say, "Right, and the score is always right, too." The volleyball parents and the athletes have been jockeying for months in order to find the best team or the best opportunities for their daughters. Many girls will tryout for multiple teams and begin a silent negotiation strategy with each team regarding their playing time, or the position they may play. (*When I was a kid, my only concern was whether I was going to find my baseball glove from last year. I had no idea that I could negotiate my position on the team.*)

The girls and their parents will evaluate the strength of the team, the strength of the players competing for their position, and the color and style of the uniforms. The uniform is more critical than you might think, as many girls "will not be caught dead wearing that uniform." I guess, at times, the uniforms clash with the color of their eyes or the style of the uniform will "make me look fat." Regardless of their particular agendas, the girls will evaluate all of this critical data before deciding which team they will honor with their presence. The parents are busy calculating the travel time to each practice and demanding that their daughter be excused from practice and road trips if it conflicts with prom, school events, or the American Idol television show.

The process is becoming so intense that, I believe, volleyball girls will soon start hiring agents to help them negotiate the best deal for the upcoming season. Right now the parents act like amateur agents. It is fun to watch parents sucking up to different coaches in order to properly position their daughter's chances of making that team. It kind of reminds me of a bunch of "old coach's groupies", who leap into action anytime a coach walks into the gym. If you have a weak stomach, this ritual is not easy to watch. Since most of the coaches are ego-maniacs, they love all the attention. I have decided to never sell my soul to the devil. I would rather my daughter earn her spot fair and square, with no politics involved. If my daughter starts believing that she can receive things in her life by Dad pulling some strings, she will never know if she has earned her position in life. I have heard of girls being cut from the team on Friday and back on the team the next Monday. It seems that sometimes Dads can pull the money-strings and perform volleyball magic. The volleyball disappear/reappear illusion is quite impressive. What a great trick! What a terrible message for the kids!

Once tryouts are over, the girls then play a bluffing game with each team they tried out for. They wait and hold off committing to any team until they have evaluated which is the best match for their personal agenda. Many girls will accept a position on one team and actually quit right before the first practice because they found a better opportunity. Some girls will just flat out lie. They will inform a team that they are accepting a position while they are still negotiating with other teams. If you have never experienced a situation like this, this process will cause you to shake your head in frustration.

At times, I don't know if I am more frustrated with the girls or the parents. I know many parents are looking for the best positions for their daughter because they see a cash return (scholarship) in the future. From my vantage point, I don't believe these teenage girls are as intense as their parents. Regardless of the driving force, the first two weeks in November in the world of club volleyball will rival any political campaign you can think of. It won't be long before we start seeing yard signs, much like political signs that read, "Select my kid for the first team." Trust me. The signs will soon be coming to a yard near you.

Since I do believe the girls will hire agents in the near future, here are a few of my humble suggestions:

1. My client would not have to report for practice if the female coach is experiencing that "time of the month." I believe it is cruel and unusual punishment for a crazy sport to be taught by crazy, unstable people.

2. My client would be permitted to eat real food while at any tournament. My client would not be forced to eat bagels and fruit while craving a "bacon, egg, and cheese biscuit." My client signed up to play volleyball, not to enter a "fat

camp." This is not an episode of *Extreme Makeover*.

3. My client would be able to leave the tournament after her final match if she is not refereeing. In the world of club volleyball, if five of the girls must stay and referee, the remaining four must stay and wait to leave with their teammates. This policy is silly. If one of your teammates must stay after school, do all the members of the team have to stay also? Of course not. This concept of a "group hug" is taken way too far. After fourteen hours in a gym, let the words of Moses prevail, "Let my people go."

4. My client would be allowed to have unsupervised visits with their parents at least twice during a tournament. If these interchanges begin to cause problems, I would allow a court reporter to transcribe the conversation "for the record." I know this may sound extreme, but sometimes we must allow parents the opportunity to act like parents. It is a wild concept, but it might just help. I have found that the girls respect their parents more than

the coach. Let the parents help clean up the emotional damage caused during the days events.

5. My client would not be allowed to participate in any cheerleading activities without receiving the standard cheerleading union pay. My client signed up for volleyball, not cheerleading.

6. My client would not be required to run laps if they are late for practice. This only applies if my client is under the legal driving limit. If my client is late because of her parents, the parents must run laps at the next tournament. These young girls don't drive. Yell at the parents; don't penalize the girls for an irresponsible parent. If their logic is correct, the volleyball parents will be better parents if they are required to run more.

7. My client would be allowed to sit whenever they are not playing. The tradition of players standing while they are not playing is clearly showing disrespect to the term "benchwarmer." If my client is to play the role of "benchwarmer", they must have the ability to honor the tradition and *sit*

down. We are even permitted to sit down in church, occasionally.

8. My client would be permitted to give the coach the "finger" if the coach is not performing up to their full coaching potential. My client would commit to using their index finger, and they would be prohibited from using any other finger, even if a different finger is warranted.

9. My client will never be permitted to take their shoes off in the car, if the travel time exceeds two hours in duration. My client acknowledges that removing her shoes, after playing volleyball for fourteen hours, is a direct violation of most clean air laws and is really a nasty thing to do to a Volleyball Dad.

10. My client will never go into the stands and fight with the fans. If my client begins making millions of dollars, just like the NBA players, she will be permitted to punch anyone she feels like at any time. Once my client earns in excess of $1 million dollars per year, she will not be responsible for her actions. Once my client turns into a professional athlete,

I promise to notify the legal system that my client will probably be visiting them in the near future.

11. My client will never be required to attend a team dinner *after* the completion of an all-day tournament. It is satanic to force parents to attend a team *bonding* dinner after they camped out in a gym for an eternity.

Volleyball Dad Lesson #17
Let our Children Grow up Slowly.

Our children grow up so fast. They are only considered "children" for a small percentage of their lives. We all know that once you become an adult, the whole world looks a little more serious and responsibilities can really weigh on us. I encourage my kids to be kids. The emotional intensity surrounding pre-teen and teenage girls playing volleyball is stunning. I have attended many fourteen-hour volleyball tournaments and very seldom do the girls look like they are having fun. I want my girls to take their assigned roles seriously and to do their best. If they lose they lose. I can't say this enough – THIS IS GIRLS' VOLLEYBALL! BACK OFF YOU HEAD-SPINNING, GREEN-VOMITING, POTTY-MOUTH, DEVIL-POSSESSED, EXORIST WANNA-BE! I think that sounds pretty close to how I feel.

So why are most parents fanatical on this sport? The answer is money or the parents are trying to recapture their own childhood experiences. First, the money issue. Due to political correctness, the NCAA is required to be aggressive with women's scholarships. This "compassion" strategy has flooded the volleyball universe with money for female athletes. Some parents are willing to sell their children into a form of volleyball-slavery for ten years if they can expect a $100,000 payoff by the time their daughter is eighteen. That's why parents have become *amateur* agents and push so hard for the right playing conditions for their daughters. I always like to ask this question when I hear about a girl receiving a college scholarship, "Who is happier, the kid or the parents?" If the answer was the parents, I know that unfortunately one young lady is going to be miserable for the next four years.

Secondly, I believe many parents are trying to recapture their childhoods. Many parents never had or were given the opportunity to participate in sports as a child. Back in the stone ages, there weren't four hundred teams, let alone team sports for girls. Participating in sports was not the cool thing to do. I believe many parents are living their sports fantasies through their childrens' lives. I know when I watch my daughters compete, it stirs up the feelings of my own sports experiences. It reminds me of a mom and daughter fighting over the daughter's wedding plans. The Mom is trying to experience the wedding she always wanted and the daughter wants to have her own wedding. Many parents choose to live their experiences through their kids. Volleyball is no different. Parents want to experience the high that they never received when they were young. Man, I'm a really deep guy!

My Volleyball Recommendations

Since no one has ever asked me for my recommendations on how to improve the game of volleyball, I want to take this opportunity to share a few volleyball thoughts for your consideration. I believe my recommendations will enhance the speed, quality, sanity and entertainment value of the game. While my recommendations will seem odd to many of you, I hope that you will, at least, give them proper consideration. Keep in mind that a true genius is never appreciated in their own time. I fear my volleyball genius status will not be appreciated until I am long-gone. Here are my top recommendations.

1. Hire blind line-judges for all matches. The calls will be the same, but everyone will at least understand why.

2. Before the match begins, tie a rope to each player. This will eliminate the constant out of rotation questions that slow down

the progress of the game. The "out of rotation" issue seems to be the number one violation that requires the High Priest to leave his/her throne. When this occurs, major delays are the result and the quality of the game suffers.

3. Eliminate timeouts when a team is up by more than ten points. It drives me crazy when a coach calls a timeout when they are losing 24-10. If a coach tries to call timeout in these situations, the coach should be required to run a lap around the court. I understand running can make someone a better coach. If running can make someone serve better, then running should make the coach coach better. Right?

4. If the High Priest must leave his/her throne during a match, everyone in the gym should receive a free soft drink to kill the time. Of course, the High Priest should pay for the drinks. I believe there must be consequences for leaving their throne and irritating the parents.

5. When the captains meet with the High Priest prior to a match, they should

have to kneel on "kneelers" like the ones found in Catholic churches. This will permit the captains to display the proper respect. It also may be a good idea to kiss the High Priest's whistle out of respect and hopefully receive a few good calls. I once attended a match where there were a few good calls.

6. If your team is able to block a kill and the ball lands out of bounds, the blocking team should receive the point. Under the current rules, when a block lands out of bounds, the blocking team loses the point. I disagree. I look at it this way. If an enemy launches a missile at the homeland and our defense system, (Patriot Missile), rejects the missile from landing in the homeland, the blockers should be rewarded, not penalized. They protected the homeland from an enemy attack. This is a stupid rule and should be changed.

7. If during a play a team allows the ball to hit the floor, the coach of that team should be required to remove a piece of clothing. The parents should have

some excitement during these marathon tournaments. I do believe the parents should reserve the right to ask a coach to put on additional clothing depending on the coach's personal appearance. This will allow the parents to participate in the volleyball activities. Since we are not allowed to talk to our daughters, we need some activity to look forward to.

8. If the score is wrong during a match, the scorekeepers must be required to stand in the middle of the court for three minutes. During these three minutes, the parents are permitted to throw volleyballs at the scorekeepers in a manner very similar to dodge-ball. I initially recommended that the parents throw wrenches as they did in the movie *Dodge-Ball*, but I concluded that the parents could hurt themselves by throwing heavy wrenches. This will allow the parents to let out a little frustration during the day. I know this sounds extreme, but there must be consequences for bad behavior or the behavior will continue. Maybe a little pain will increase the focus of the scorekeepers. If

my wife could have released some of her frustration in this manner, she probably would not have lost her mind in Atlanta. I'm just trying to help bring a little sanity into the insane asylum.

9. If a player forgets their uniform, they should be required to wear a shirt that says, "I forgot my volleyball shirt and my name. Do you know me? Please make sure I arrive home safely."

10. If a player serves the ball into the net, one of the player's parents must run a lap around the court. I understand running will help our daughters serve better.

11. The concept of "Volleyball Buddies" should be made illegal. For those of you that are unfamiliar with the tradition, let me explain. At the beginning of the volleyball crusades, players are assigned to be "Volleyball Buddies" with several other players. The player is required to buy presents, or *junk in a bag*, for a fellow teammate. Usually, at ten o'clock at night, my daughter will say "Oh no – tomorrow is *junk in a bag* day for volleyball." My wife will then jump into her car and head

to the store. She will buy a few pieces of candy, a pencil and a bottle of Ritalin, just in case the player is required to keep score at the match. (Of course, the bottle of Ritalin was my idea.) This tradition is a tremendous burden on the parents and should be discontinued. You can't force volleyball girls to be buddies. It's best to just let life happen. It usually works out pretty well that way.

Oops! That Can't Be Good

This next story is true. I have decided to protect the identity of this individual for obvious reasons. For pure entertainment value, I have decided to tell this story in the first-person. It just reads better. I hope you enjoy!

There are moments in everyone's life when the unspeakable happens. It may be a terrible accident, illness or business tragedy. This next story is *not* about any of those moments. However, it is about an unspeakable event that happened to me during one of our volleyball road trips. It is very embarrassing but also very funny. I believe it is healthy to laugh at ourselves. This episode is so painful that it is only now that I can speak and laugh about it.

It started out as a normal volleyball Saturday. Our team was headed to Louisville, Kentucky for an all day volleyball tournament. We arrived a little late, and we only had a few minutes before my daughter's match was to begin. I informed Barb that I needed to run to the restroom before the match as I consumed two giant Diet Cokes, which I called the "urinaters" during our trip. As I hustled to the restroom and assumed my position at the standing urinal, the unthinkable happened. I decided to release some of the excess carbonation I had consumed from my Diet Cokes. Much to my surprise, the carbonation release was not in the form of a gas but released in the form of a solid. Yes, I crapped in my pants. Since this was my first experience with this situation, I panicked and ran into one of the stalls. Let me make a brief observation for you. This solid release was extremely hot and I now appreciate it when a baby cries after the number two process. It was very uncomfortable and I wanted to cry like a baby at that moment.

As I stood in the stall and contemplated suicide, I decided a major cleanup was needed. It may not have been the size of the "Fernald nuclear waste cleanup", but to me it was a serious sanitation issue. Upon my initial evaluation, several of my garments were goners. I quickly disposed of what I could and began the cleanup. It is important to note that I have three daughters and I have never changed a single diaper in my life. I know this may sound unbelievable but it is the truth. Now I am faced with literally changing my own diaper. When I finally secure enough nerve and I felt I didn't stink like Tommy the Turd, I left the scene of the accident. I definitely left the restroom in a worst condition than when I found it.

Since I was gone so long, Barb asked me, "Are you alright?" I said, "No." I found it very difficult to explain to my wife what I had done at the age of forty. I whispered to Barb, "I crapped in my pants and I need to go to Kmart in order to replace my garments that gave their life during the ordeal." I now consider that statement as one of the worst statements you could ever say to your wife. I honestly would rather tell her I had cancer than to admit to a total body breakdown in my muscular structure. After my daughter's match that seemed to take forever, we bolted to Kmart. Yes, Barb did sit in the back seat with the window open. I felt like an idiot and smelled like a baby-changing clinic. I told you earlier, if you hang around club volleyball long enough you will experience some very bizarre events. I just never thought I would be at the epicenter of the chaos.

Volleyball Dad Lesson # 18
It's Okay to Laugh at Yourself.

If there is one life lesson I have mastered, it is that I am willing to share my screw-ups with the world. Take this story as an example. My family has had violent arguments concerning this chapter. My wife thinks I'm insane to share such a story and my girls appreciate the humor. If you are reading this, I guess my girls prevailed.

I encourage everyone to laugh at life, especially your life. Since we were not created perfect, we are definitely going to do stupid things in our lives. If you are willing to laugh at yourself, life could be fun instead of a bad soap opera.

Volleyball Dad Lesson # 19
Always Expect the Unexpected.

As the commercial says, "Life can come at you very fast." If you expect the unexpected, you will realize that life just happens and you must deal with the hand you are dealt. If you never anticipate the unexpected you will be shocked and angry when life's unexpected moments happen. You will probably spend too much time whining and complaining about the moment. Just accept life and move on. I know it is easier said than done, but what choices do we really have. Life can be challenging. We just need to be a little tougher than life. I now carry extra garments in my trunk at all times, just in case lighting does strike twice.

20 Life Strategies from a Volleyball Dad to All Volleyball Girls

I love giving advice. I normally don't follow my own advice, but I still love giving it to the world. This is really good stuff, and I hope to follow most of these strategies at some point in my life.

1. Have a "No Excuse" Mentality. Never make excuses for the choices in your life. The "dog ate my homework" excuse didn't work in school and it definitely will not work in the adult world. Too many people in the world today regularly attend pity parties. Never attend a pity party unless your last name is *Pity*. If you did not understand that last sentence, please send a note to your local school district and ask for your money back.

2. Results Matter. Too many people believe that trying matters. While trying is important, generating results will determine the course of your life. Take this simple test. Right now *try* and scratch your nose. I mean I want you to *try* really hard. Isn't it a fact that you either succeeded in scratching your nose or you failed to scratch your nose? There is no such thing as *trying*. You only succeed or fail on your choices in life.

3. You Will Become Who You Hang With. If you hang with losers and whiners you will *become* a loser and whiner. Have you ever noticed how drunks, drug addicts and bums hang together? Pick your friends wisely. They are a reflection of who you will be. It is better to be a loner than hang with idiots.

4. Small Decisions Generate Large Results. When you take your first drink, you are on your way. You may not be an alcoholic, but you have taken the first step. I know that making bad eating decisions seems like a small thing, but trust me, a heart attack is a big thing. Your first "experiment" with drugs will lead you to a lab. It will then lead you to a prison.

5. Character Matters My definition of character is to simply do what is right when no one is watching. It doesn't take character to do the right thing when someone is watching but *can* you do the right thing when someone *isn't* watching? Your employers will pay you handsomely if you are a person of character. I have been in a leadership position for over thirty years, and I would pay you handsomely if I did not need to be your baby-sitter. I classify people at work as H.M. or L.M. The H.M. stands for a "high-maintenance" person who is someone you must watch all day. The L.M. is a "low-maintenance" person who is someone you don't need to watch all day. The L.M. will always earn at least 25% more money than a H.M. person. The irony of this reality is that the H.M. person will never understand why they are paid less for the same duties. If you know a few H.M. people, I suggest you buy this book for them and maybe this section will smack them in the face. If it doesn't help, I just want to say thanks for buying my book.

6. *Your Words Matter*. Do your words matter to anyone? If you give someone your word can they count on it? If you say you will pick someone up at 5 p.m., do you arrive on time? If someone catches you in a lie, do you realize that they will put a big question mark on everything you say for the rest of your relationship? Choose your words wisely. The world will judge you by how often your words reflect your actions.

7. *Mom and Dad are not Your Enemies*. Someday you will appreciate the fact that someone really cares about your health and safety. The world can be a tough place at times. You will long for the days when someone cared where you were. Many people will live their entire lives praying that they will find someone who will love and care for them. Right now, those people are your parents.

8. Learn from Your Parents, Don't Imitate Them. Learn the best your parents have to offer and ignore the rest. Parents are not perfect, so don't expect them to be. If your parents only offer 75% of the good stuff, accept the 75% and eliminate the remaining 25%. Just because your parents may be alcoholics, you don't have to be. Develop your own filtering system that will only allow the good stuff to filter through. The quality of your life is your choice alone.

9. It's Okay to be a Quitter. At anytime, you can choose to quit smoking, drinking, doing drugs, having sex, eating badly, hanging with human debris, drinking Pepsi, and saying "like" ten times in every sentence. It may sound impossible, but it can be done. There are many people *like* you that *like* can change *like* at any time *like* do you know what I mean? (Did you catch the dripping sarcasm in the last sentence?)

10. Daily Disciplines are the Key to a Great Life. If you can commit to a daily program, you will be happy. Stop! Reread that sentence and really take that statement as profound. If you consume 1,500 calories a day you will not have a weight problem. I could put down 1,500 calories at breakfast. If you will take a sheet of paper and write down your daily commitments that you will follow for the rest of your life, you will live in a special place. You are in control of your identity. So who do you want to be?

11. You Will Get What You Deserve in Life, Not What You Need. I need good health, but I don't deserve good heath. This is a universal law of life. You "sow what you reap." Many people in our society *need* money but they really don't *deserve* more money. They did not commit to obtaining an education. They do not want to start at the bottom and work their way up the ladder. Most people want to start at the top, but life does not work that way. That is why so many people play the lottery. They hope they will hit it big by being lucky rather than being hard-working. Even after you leave school, you will find that your education will never stop. I currently read two to three business books a month to keep up with the rest of the business world. I have been competing in the business world for thirty years. I think I only read four books during my formal sixteen educational years. Keep reading and learning. Since most people will stop learning after their formal schooling is complete, you can really have a big advantage in the marketplace by continuing to grow. Employers will always pay for knowledge.

12. Don't Put Lipstick on a Pig. I am constantly frustrated by people who pretend to be something that they are not. I know this sounds negative, but many people are not what they seem. They pretend to be honest people and they lie, cheat and steal. They want you to believe that they care for you when they only care for themselves. If you are a pig (bad person) at least be honest about it. Proudly tell the world that you are a pig. Don't pretend to be someone you are not. Eventually, everyone will figure it out. I am a sarcastic honest idiot, and I am proud of it!

13. You have More Talent than You Realize. Most of us will go to our grave and only use 10% of our God-given ability. Try new things and push yourself out of your comfort zone. At age fifty-one, I took my first dance lesson. Talk about being out of my element. I really believe that open-heart surgery was more enjoyable. Do you know anyone who is "going to do something" and for some reason they never do it? Be a do-er, not a talker. If you say you are going to climb that mountain, go out and buy some climbing shoes. I said I was going to write a stupid book about a Volleyball Dad and I did it. What are you going to do?

14. Things Don't Cost Too Much, I Don't Make Enough Money. – I heard this statement many years ago by Jim Rohn, a motivational speaker. It has stuck with me during my business career. If you know people who are buying and doing things you want to do, maybe you don't make enough money. Don't complain about how expensive something is, start committing to being excellent in your career. Make sure you inform your boss that you want to be the number one at whatever you do at work and start making it happen today. If you are cashier, be the number one cashier. If you are a waitress, sales executive, vice-president or president, make sure you focus on being the number one at everything you do. I would estimate that 80% of our population focuses on doing the least amount of work in order to maintain their employment. If you do the opposite, the executives at your place of employment will notice you.

15. If You Want to Make Millions, Dress Like a Million Dollars. – I believe our society has deteriorated over the past forty years. The casual day nonsense is everywhere. It seems many people prefer to look like they are homeless or members of a gang. I have found it difficult to pay the bills with this look in the business community. If you want to be noticed at work, dress as if you *deserve* to be noticed. Always dress 10% better than everyone you work with. This will be very easy to do in America today. My family recently spent the evening viewing pictures from my childhood. What really impressed me about the pictures was the way my brothers and sister were dressed in every picture. We were always dressed "to the nines." (That means we were dressed very well.) We looked like we were going to church, a wedding or funeral in every picture. When I look at our more current pictures of the holidays, I notice that many people are in jeans and tee shirts. When did society conclude that poor dress was appropriate for *all* occasions? I once heard someone ask their spouse, "Are my good jeans clean?" I know we have fallen far when we have jeans for church, dinner, movie, work and dating. If you want to be a star, start dressing like one.

16. Solve Problems, Build a Career. – Learn this reality and learn it well. An employer's primary reason for hiring you is – *To Solve Their Problems*. They don't care about your personal agenda, your dog, the hours you want to work or numerous causes. Everyone has a cause and yours is not any better than your co-workers. Employers want you to solve a business problem and improve the quality of their business life. The majority of the world will never grasp this concept. If you are on an interview and an employer asks you the following question, "What type of work are you looking for?" Your answer should be, "My goal is to have the opportunity to make your business problems disappear. Is that something that would benefit you?" Most employers will probably sob uncontrollably. Be sure to take plenty of tissues in order to solve the employer's crying problem.

17. Learn to Walk Fast. – I have a theory that it is impossible to work faster than you walk. After I interview a candidate for a position at our company, I always try and observe them walking to their car after the interview. I believe that someone's speed of foot is in direct correlation to their productivity speed. Spend some time and observe your friends and see if you come to the same conclusion.

18. Write Down Your Success Formulas. – You should live your life based on your own formulas. I have found that all successful people follow a success routine. I bet you follow the same routine when you shower and prepare to take on the world. I know I do. I shower, apply deodorant, blow-dry my nine hairs, brush my teeth, shave, put on my socks, shirt, suit pants, belt, tie and then my suit jacket. I proceed to kiss my wife on the forehead and head for the office. I follow the exact routine everyday without exception. We are creatures of habit. Work on your success habits everyday. It seems that some people work on the wrong habits every day. Every day we choose to reinforce positive habits or negative habits.

19. Get Even with People Who Have Helped You. – Someone has made a positive impact in your life. Think of five special people and send them a hand-written thank you note. Today! Trust me. It will make their day - maybe their decade.

20. Thank God Every Day That You Live in the United States of America. – We are truly blessed to have freedom and opportunity. Too many people take our country for granted. I was recently at the famous Fort Mitchell 4th of July parade. I observed an elderly man around eighty years old struggle to stand when he saw the American flag approaching. He stood and saluted. He then quietly sat down. At the same time I noticed hundreds of kids and parents wrestling on the ground to secure the free penny-candy that was thrown from the parade participants. I have often wondered what that eighty-year-old proud American thought at that moment. I have a feeling he was thinking, "I'm starting to worry if America is losing its focus on what the cost of freedom really is. We seem to be drifting to a country of more and more penny-candy beggars." Please honor America and don't take our freedoms for granted. Earn your rewards, don't *beg* for them.

A Touching Message For All Volleyball Dads

Let me take this opportunity to thank you for allowing me to vent a little, maybe a lot, and share a few thoughts about the crazy world of club volleyball and life. I know I was pretty brutal at times throughout this book. However, I have been put through hell and this book is my only means to fight back. I know each of you could write your own book about your club volleyball experiences or other team sports. I hope you do. Many people have asked me if it has helped my mental health to vent my frustrations with the world of volleyball. Unfortunately, the answer is no. I believe the scars are permanently embedded for all time. I have decided to use my one question, at the time of my death, to ask God, "What was the point of putting me and my family through all of that volleyball stress?" I'm going to be pretty upset if He doesn't have a great reason. I know that last comment may prevent me from being able to ask that one question, but wish me luck, because I do plan on asking it.

I would like to ask all Volleyball Dads to do me one special favor when you finish reading this book. Immediately, after you tell one thousand of your friends to buy this book, by going to www.TomWurtz.com, go find your volleyball daughter, or any of your children, and look them in the eye and say,

"I love you. This world is full of obstacles, challenges and downright crazy people. I know that because I am one of the crazy ones. I want you to know that while there is still life in this body, I will help you deal with life, if you let me. I have spent many years in the world of volleyball showing you my commitment and unconditional love. I have driven in snow storms, terrible rain storms and I have even tolerated hate speech. (My youngest daughter once told me I looked like Danny DeVito. I don' know if that statement qualifies as hate-speech but I know my self-esteem will never be the same.) Please allow me to continue to be there for you throughout your life. Just because I'm no longer sitting in the stands, I am as committed as ever to just being your Dad. Whatever life has planned for you, please remember, I will always be in the stands cheering you on. I once heard that every time a whistle blows, a Volleyball Dad

gets his wings. I believe I have earned my wings. Whenever you need me, I will be there because I am a Volleyball Dad and that is what Volleyball Dads do."

6515938R00072

Made in the USA
San Bernardino, CA
11 December 2013